"Steve has a great gift of v   :o
something with which Go   it
to know how to best under   __   _ _ ....lg
resource to its full, then reading this will greatly benefit you."

Paul Harcourt – Vicar of All Saints' Woodford Wells and National
Leader, New Wine England.

"Both accessible and practical, Steve's writing is a real help in
understanding what God says through the Bible."

Steve Maltz – Founder of Foundations Conferences, Saltshaker Web
Community and Saffron Planet Radio; author of over twenty books
including 'Livin' the Life' and 'Into the Lion's Den.'

"John's Gospel is unfathomable, in the sense that those who study and
reflect on it know that there is always more. John, the writer was fully
aware of this too! To explore it using the lens of time throws new
light on the Gospel as a whole, as well as the passages on which
Stephen focuses.

In this telling of the Good News of Jesus the Christ, eternity and
time intersect. In Jesus, the eternal Word indwells humanity and
therefore time. Judging when the time was right was critical in the
mission of Jesus. It was not right at the wedding in Cana of Galilee
(chapter 2:4), but it was in Jerusalem when some Greeks sought him
out (chapter 12:23). And using the context provided by the Jewish
Scriptures and the New Testament it is possible to see that the whole
of his life was lived at the time that the Father knew was right
(Galatians 4: 4).

As creatures of time we tend to take it for granted for most of our
lives, but it is of critical importance to understanding God's work in
his world and in our lives. T.S. Eliot began what many consider to be
his greatest work with a profound observation about how present
time relates to both the past and the future. Redemption means that

in some way time works backwards; hope, that the present and the past are contained in future time (*Four Quartets, Burnt Norton, I*). And Albert Einstein opened our eyes to the relativity of time and space. So Steve is in good company in realising that an exploration of time is likely to be a journey of surprising, if not amazing discoveries.

I warmly commend this book for its faithfulness to the Gospel of John, its down to earth examples (well befitting a Leyton Orient supporter), and its openness to the way God works in and through time."

Dr Keith J White – Director of Mill Grove, London; Lecturer at Spurgeon's College; author of several books including 'The art of faith,' 'A place for us,' 'In the meantime,' 'In His image'.

TWO MINUTES ADDED ON

STEPHEN BISHOP

Zaccmedia

Published by Zaccmedia
www.zaccmedia.com
info@zaccmedia.com

Published June 2018

ISBN: 978-1-911211-83-9

British Library Cataloguing-in-Publication Data
A catalogue record for this book is available from the British Library.

CONTENTS

1

INTRODUCTION: HOPE AND A SECOND CHANCE

What are the similarities between a job interview, a chance meeting with a celebrity, and a first date? There may be several – or none. These may have been situations you've had to face – or not. But I suggest if we have had to handle the aftermath of such face-to-face encounters then each of them can leave us coming away with a realisation. This is that we missed an opportunity to say something that could have made a big impact. Now, however, the chance has gone, possibly never to be repeated. That's been my experience, probably the result of not being one of the world's quickest thinkers! So after these events (sadly, more than one) I would re-run those conversations in my mind and reflect on the replies that never emerged.

Of course, one of the key aspects in respect of 'time' is that we cannot go backwards and add to, or amend, words that we have spoken. This also applies to things we could have done but didn't, or did do but probably should not have done. Those words and actions, done or undone, will remain... along with regrets.

QUESTIONS

Circumstances such as those described above can make us all too conscious of the fact that we are trapped in time. It is a non-negotiable element of all that we do and plan. It is the 'full stop' beyond which we cannot exert control. No one is exempt. The billionaire has to work to exactly the same 24 hours as someone receiving social security benefit.

But there is more. Time forces us to face up to questions that can have a deep impact. Is it too late? How long is left? Is it possible to make up for lost time? If I knew then what I know now, would I have said something different? Have I missed the opportunity?

Do these questions and the situations they represent mean that we are hopelessly at the mercy of time? Even more importantly, does a belief in God in any way affect this whole scenario? Some of these aspects were explored in a previous book that I authored: *Time: Full Stop or Question Mark?* It wasn't pretending to resolve all the issues or provide complete answers. This was just as well because my mind continued to 'orbit' this subject... and realise that there were further important 'angles' to consider!

FREEDOM

In particular it became even clearer that Jesus, in His interaction with people as described in the Gospel accounts, was very aware of the 'time' element affecting those around Him. Even more striking were the ways in which, either openly or less obviously, time was an aspect that did not control or constrain His intervention. Indeed Jesus showed that He was Master of every element of life (and death), including time.

This freedom which Jesus enjoyed with regard to time did not only have very practical and dramatic consequences for those who encountered Him during His ministry on earth. The implications of Jesus as Lord of lords and King of kings, the Alpha and Omega as relating to time, are very relevant to us today. For that reason we can have a real basis for hope in situations affected by time that are outside our control. We do not have to be at the mercy of the ticking clock.

The following pages therefore look at what is described in the Bible. Christians believe that it is not simply an amazing and insightful piece of literature. It's also seen as having a life-changing dynamic that touches us deeply. There's a particular verse which states that God's Word, the Bible, is 'alive and active ['quick and powerful', KJV]' (Hebrews 4:12). Perhaps we should not be surprised that, as we read it, we start to see ourselves and our situations in a different light.

APPLICATION

The Bible also explains that even when we are struggling to understand what it's saying, God helps us to grasp the 'bigger picture'. The psalmist stated: 'The unfolding of your words gives light; it gives understanding to the simple' (Psalm 119:130). This means that we can start to see what God says in the Bible being applicable to us personally. But such insight is not instantaneous; it's a work in progress. It's not surprising, therefore, to find that there's a great deal more for us to explore and learn about God's angle on the subject of time – as I found!

3

'ADDED ON'

The title of this particular book, *Two Minutes Added On*, is derived from a sporting term. More specifically it relates to professional football (soccer) matches where a fourth official has been closely monitoring the game from the touchline as it has progressed. He or she has been particularly noting when time has been taken up by events outside the flow of the game. This, for instance, would take into account the time taken for an injured player to receive attention, or other interruptions. After adding up these 'stoppages', the official holds up a board showing the consequent amount of time to be added on to the normal playing period so as to compensate for this calculated loss. The board is normally illuminated, made visible to the referee, players, coaching staff and spectators.

It's generally reckoned that such an 'added on' period would be somewhere between one and five minutes. However, if your team is losing 3–0 (sadly, with my local side, not an uncommon scoreline) then the amount of 'added on' time is purely academic. Not a lot is going to change in those few moments. But if the score is 0–0 or 1–0, for instance, then that short time can be crucial. Even struggling Leyton Orient (that's my team, based in east London) have been known to score (or concede) a goal in that brief 'window'.

GOD: THE FINAL SAY

Time may not be set in stone and unalterable as we may think. As previously outlined, God's work is not constrained in an unyielding timeframe. That football official may be responsible for calculating and then indicating the amount of time to be added on. But the final judgement as to when the whistle is blown to end the match is down solely to the referee. As we shall be seeing, God is the final arbiter as to when time is up. He can seem to add on time in our situations. It is He who also says when no more time is left.

HOPE

The accounts of Jesus in the Gospels are particularly relevant with regard to showing how God works in this way. John, whose Gospel is the source of the miracles examined in the main section of this book, records Jesus as specifically saying: 'For I have come down from heaven not to do my will but to do the will of him who sent me' (John 6:38). His actions were determined by God His Father, not by time. Each of the seven miraculous 'signs' that are described in that Gospel are explored in this book in order to determine the element of time that emerges... and that applies to us (see Chapters 3–9).

Forming a foundation to those seven chapters is Chapter 2 which focuses on a miracle recorded by each of the other Gospel writers. This is the account of the healing of the paralysed man. It clearly shows that Jesus was prepared to 'make time' for people. It's an attitude that undergirds each of those accounts in John's Gospel that are subsequently examined. Looking at these accounts should give us a sense of hope and peace arising from the power of God in ruling over time's boundaries.

The three concluding 'Postscripts' are intended to be a 'launch pad'. They show us that we also, like the Christians in the early Church (as described in the Acts of the Apostles on which those Postscripts are based), can take practical steps to personally experience God move outside our conception of time.

An expanded 'Reflection' section concludes each chapter to help work through the material by way of personal meditation and, particularly, small group discussion.

A SECOND CHANCE

But a concluding comment. It arises from a particular role that I had to play when working in the civil service. This required me to represent my department at public hearings. Although these were not high-profile occasions, they were overseen by a legally qualified chairperson who would adjudicate on the cases put before them. However, they could also involve the presence of a professional representative (such as a solicitor or welfare rights expert) acting on behalf of their client who had raised a grievance against the department. So although I undertook a considerable amount of research in preparing for those hearings, there was always the likelihood of me being questioned by a sharp-minded advocate. Did I mention that I'm not a quick thinker? This scenario was therefore a daunting one to contemplate!

But although in the face of any interrogation there was the possibility of me failing to give adequate answers, all was not lost! Towards the end of any hearing there was the opportunity for me to take a breath and retrieve the situation. I could either 'clarify' my initial answers or, indeed, raise a salient point which had not previously been covered for the chairperson to take into account. This was because that same chairperson would inevitably turn to me and ask if I had any final comments. Time would therefore be given for me to recapture any lost opportunity. Knowing that this would be part of the procedure meant that I was slightly more relaxed. I knew that there would, in time, arise a second chance.

work (covering a whole spectrum of scenarios), together with training and education, can be so important. These can all contribute to a right sense of self-worth and value. But it doesn't always happen... or at least it shouldn't be assumed as an automatic experience. My own employment situation dramatically deteriorated – alongside that of many colleagues – when a different style of management was introduced in the high-profile government department in which I was working. The emphasis that was placed wholly on targets, performance figures and 'buzz' meetings completely changed the work culture. Whether this was intentional or not was difficult to judge. The remoteness of managers and their reluctance or unavailability to discuss factors behind this all-consuming focus on numbers compounded the situation. It added to the sense that I and others had that actually we no longer counted and were now simply cyphers lost in a big organisation.

A CROWD... AND A PROBLEM

So, when Jesus was confronted by someone who didn't really 'count', being generally unwanted and lost in a vast crowd, what was His response? To answer that question it's important to notice the setting in which this situation arose. The Gospel accounts are, of course, full of descriptions showing Jesus in action. He was healing the sick, delivering the demonised, raising the dead, providing for those in need and, in all of this, showing God's care and concern for people. But as part of this action He gave a lot of time to preaching, teaching, talking and instruction. Those to whom He spoke in this way included His disciples, the wider group of followers, the marginalised, the community at large and the Jewish religious leaders.

The many different groups listening to Jesus had their various 'agendas'. Sadly these were not all positive ones. So when Luke described a particular occasion when Jesus was preaching (according to Matthew and Mark, Jesus was in his 'home' town of Capernaum; Matthew 9:1; Mark 2:1), he distinctly recorded some of those who were in the audience. They were the 'Pharisees and teachers of the law', who had come from Jerusalem, along with other people who 'had come from every village of Galilee and from Judea' (Luke 5:17). This was a noticeably large crowd squeezing inside a house, as Mark explained: 'They gathered in such large numbers that there was no room left, not even outside the door' (Mark 2:2).

LATERAL THINKING

The venue for that meeting may not have involved quite as many people as those using London Waterloo, but it clearly presented a problem to a small group. These four men were carrying a fifth, paralysed and lying on a mat. Their intention was to bring him to Jesus so that he could be healed. However, the existence of the crowd meant that the normal means of access through the door was not an option. 'Lateral thinking' (or divine inspiration) kicked in. The roof of the one-storey house was accessed... and opened up. The man on the mat was then lowered through the resultant hole, right in front of Jesus (see Luke 5:19).

JESUS STOPPED...

It's at this point that the 'time' element emerged... being very relevant both to this paralysed man and to us. Three aspects are interwoven into this account. The first was that as soon as the paralysed man was lowered in front of Him, Jesus stopped what

He was doing. He stopped His teaching and preaching. He stopped focusing on that audience in the packed house which included those high-profile religious leaders. Jesus stopped to give the invalid His full and complete attention. In doing this – and as subsequently evidenced by His words and attitude – He conveyed a clear non-verbal message: 'I've got time for you.'

This action was not only an amazing one at that time. The religious leaders were subsequently to complain that Jesus gave His time to tax collectors and 'sinners' (see Luke 15:1). But it remains something that Jesus still does today. In that connection few of us seem to cope very well with unexpected interruptions, especially

> Jesus ... 'I've got time for you'

when we are in 'full flow'... particularly when the phone rings as we are eating a meal or sitting in front of our favourite TV show. Even in the work environment I recall the unanimous groan that would erupt in my office when the fire alarm was sounded (always in practice mode) and we would be required to instantly stop our work and move outside. On these occasions our minds are almost inevitably still dwelling on the television, plate of food, or computer data with which we want to reconnect. But not Jesus! On that occasion, whatever was on His teaching schedule, preaching notes or 'power point' presentation, He stopped. He shut out everything else in order to give time to this paralysed man.

The fact that Jesus projected this message – 'I've got time for you' – is especially relevant to us. In an age when, on occasions, we can feel unwanted, unnoticed and isolated – even in a crowd of people such as in London Waterloo – these are powerful words. They form the bedrock of what we read in the Bible

13

concerning God's intervention in this world. This is illustrated by what He said through the Old Testament prophet:

> So do not fear, for I am with you;
> do not be dismayed, for I am your God.
> I will strengthen you and help you;
> I will uphold you with my righteous right
> hand.

(Isaiah 41:10)

That unspoken but clear message of Jesus is also important to us because we know that people around us can be so busy. They have schedules, appointments, other responsibilities and pressing demands on their time. This means they simply haven't got time – or much of it – to give to others, especially when no advance warning is given either by text or email. People nowadays rarely 'drop everything' to give us their time. But here was Jesus, who stopped His teaching, didn't worry about the clock, and gave this paralysed man time and attention.

...THE MEN SENSED...
Secondly the four men, and possibly the paralysed man himself, sensed a 'time' element relating to their situation. They did not, it seems, have any hesitation in adopting this somewhat unorthodox means by which to bring the sick man to Jesus. This possibly arose because of the man's condition. As time progressed it was clearly not going to improve but almost certainly deteriorate, taking into account the lack of medical knowledge in that age. But there was also the situation of Jesus' own movement and ministry. He was travelling around the towns and villages preaching, teaching and healing. So although on this

occasion He was in Capernaum it would not have been clear how long that was to be the case. Who knows whether, when the current teaching session was completed, Jesus and His disciples might immediately move on, or find a quiet place for prayer and rest? The fact these men faced was that help was needed *now*. The account by Luke underlines an element that may have particularly galvanised them: 'And the power of the Lord was with Jesus to heal those who were ill' (Luke 5:17).

So, by reason of these background details, the men realised that no time was to be lost. For them it was not so much a case of seeing a 'window of opportunity' as a 'roof of opportunity'! They therefore did not delay in coming to Jesus with their need. This also applies to us. Coming to Jesus does not require us to book an appointment, go online to allocate a 'slot', or send an email request. We do not have to wait until the next Sunday service or home-group meeting. We can come to Jesus at any time, day or night, and at any point during the week. He is able and willing to welcome us.

...AND JESUS MADE 'SPACE'

Lastly this account is clear in showing that Jesus, in addressing the paralysed man's spiritual and physical needs, gave him as much time as was necessary. First, Jesus saw the man's deep and vital need, which led Him to pronounce: 'Friend, your sins are forgiven' (Luke 5:20). Then, after making some pointed comments to the religious leaders who were observing, Jesus pronounced physical restoration: 'I tell you, get up, take your mat and go home' (Luke 5:24). There was an immediate result. The man stood up in front of everyone, picked up his mat, and went home praising God.

There was no hint or suggestion that Jesus was in a hurry, needed to get back to His teaching, and could only allocate a few moments to this paralysed man. He made 'space' for him, giving him all the time that was required in order to bring wholeness of spirit and body. In our own age this often does not happen. There seem to be so many constraints on people's time that it is 'rationed'. This means, for example, that there are prescribed time constraints for counselling sessions, speed dating, and performance reviews at work. All of these, and many other situations, can involve commitment to a set time period. This may be helpful in ensuring that conversations are focused. But it may equally stifle unforeseen and productive discussion.

He made 'space' for him

On one occasion I attended a workshop for would-be writers. The person leading these sessions allocated each delegate just five minutes in a one-to-one meeting, during which we could 'sell' our project. This proposition was another occasion when my limitations in 'thinking on my feet' were challenged! It was also, I thought, pretty futile. It was a 'production line' process which contributed nothing towards building a rapport or facilitating constructive discussion. In sharing the situation with other delegates it seemed that we were all given the same advice anyway – to put our proposal in writing and send it by email for further consideration. I didn't waste any further time!

How much this contrasts with Jesus! Wherever we read of Him in the Gospels He was always giving people as much time as they wanted. He never curtailed the time spent with someone who genuinely wanted His help or needed His attention – even those to whom others would not 'give the time of day', being unnoticed and lost in the crowd. He commended Mary of

Bethany for wanting to spend time with Him and listen to what He said (Luke 10:38–42). So the next time you are in a large crowd – perhaps even London Waterloo – remember that each person you observe is someone for whom Jesus wants to give time. And that includes you.

* * *

REFLECTION

Grounds for hope (as seen in this chapter):

- Jesus wanted to spend time with people who were 'ordinary', also the marginalised.
- He was willing to be interrupted, stopping what He was doing.
- He gave time to the paralysed man.
- He also gave as much time and space as necessary to intervene in this man's spiritual and physical conditions, enabling forgiveness and healing to be brought.

POINTS TO PONDER

1. How well do you cope with interruptions and unexpected interference to your schedule/routine or planned arrangements? Tick as many boxes as apply.

   Always badly ☐
   It depends on who is interrupting ☐
   It depends on how I'm interrupted ☐
   It varies, depending on how pressured I am ☐
   I welcome interruptions ☐

2. What factors affect your reaction to interruptions as shown in the boxes you have ticked?
3. Jesus made time for this paralysed man. What does it show us about Jesus when we realise that He was not put off by interruptions?
4. What other examples are there in the Gospels of Jesus not being fazed when interrupted?
5. How does it affect your relationship with Jesus to know that He wants to make time to be available for you and that there are no constraints as to when this is?

3

GOD'S 'TIME ZONE'

'Woman, why do you involve me?' Jesus replied. 'My hour has not yet
come.'

(John 2:4)

Read: John 2:1–12

Train journeys are straightforward, aren't they? But when I
checked the internet about travelling from London to North
Wales I discovered that such a trip was definitely not in that
'straightforward' category! The screen showed three trains and
two changes. Even before embarking on the mainline, I would
need to negotiate the London Underground. This whole enter-
prise was not looking good. Delays of any description could
wreck the entire schedule. Also needing to be factored in was the
question of locating the different platforms for successive depar-
tures. At least I was able to glean those details from the internet

and find out where I needed to be, and how to get there... which I fortunately managed to achieve at each point, eventually getting to my final destination. On this occasion the trains had kept to their advertised times – just!

It was actually this vital element of timing that instigated action leading to a far wider impact than just the railways. Prior to the introduction of trains in Britain, the issue of 'local time' was exactly as described in that term. Each city, town and locality more or less set its own time, dependent upon their observations of the sun's rising and setting. People and produce did not tend to travel very far or fast. So the need for accurate and uniform 'time' did not arise. However, the Industrial Revolution changed the situation dramatically. Running trains effectively, especially from east to west, required a standard time to be adopted by the railways. Timetables and interchanging were based on the same time throughout the network, enabled by the use of electric telegraph signals to broadcast the time as determined at Greenwich. This was the reason for railway stations incorporating high and prominent clock towers in their structure. The clocks clearly displayed the time to which they were working, irrespective of what 'time' it was (or wasn't) in the locality around them. However, it required an Act of Parliament (in 1880) to ensure that standard time was recorded across the country, enabling each area to show the same time on the clock.

DIFFERENT 'TIME ZONE'

Time continues to be an integral part of our actions and planning. It necessitates ongoing awareness of our 'time' as being accurate according to our location. Airline passengers and those journeying between continents, even adjacent countries, know the importance of this aspect of travel. This includes, for instance, adjusting watches by one hour to take into account 'British Summer Time'. In the springtime the clocks go forward ('spring' forward) and in the autumn they go back ('fall' back). Of course, the weather often fails to adjust to the 'summertime' under which everything else is now operating, often obstinately producing wintry conditions! Across in the USA the broad expanse of territory necessitates the provision of four 'time zones' extending from 'Eastern' to 'Pacific'.

One of the many changes that take place when we embark on a life of following Jesus as Christians is that we move into a different 'time zone'. But do not be alarmed! This is not referring to any further adjustment to our watches, or moving in a 'parallel universe'. It simply means needing to be alert to God's timing, rather than solely regulating our actions according to past practices or following everyone else's attitude towards time.

A DISASTER

This way of operating was particularly shown by Jesus when He performed His first recorded miracle. John's Gospel describes Jesus and His disciples being guests at a marriage at Cana in Galilee. At some point a social disaster occurred: the supply of wine began to run out. Whether any other action was taken to replenish supplies is not disclosed. John simply records that eventually Mary, Jesus' mother, went to her son and stated: 'They have no more wine.' To this Jesus replied: 'Woman, why do you involve me? ... My hour has not yet come' (John 2:3, 4).

In speaking those words Jesus was indicating awareness of another schedule that was in operation. It took priority over any pressing physical and obvious needs. The word 'hour' that He used simply referred to the time shown on the clock or to a general period. So, rather than being wholly occupied with the present situation that seemed to demand immediate action, Jesus was working to another timetable. This was a spiritual one that took into account God's overall plan of salvation, leading to Jesus going to the cross. An integral part of that plan was Jesus revealing Himself to be God's only Son. John's Gospel was written with that in mind. The writer picked out seven miracles (from among a huge number) which Jesus performed, and included them in his narrative in order to underline the deity of Christ. These miracles were described as 'signs' (see John 2:11; 3:2; 4:48; 6:2; 6:14; 6:26; 6:30; 12:37; 20:30). Their purpose of showing Jesus to be God was termed as 'revealing' His 'glory' (see John 1:14; 2:11).

KNOWING OUR TIMETABLE

Jesus was aware of time. This fact was reflected all through His ministry and is actually a feature that can bring encouragement to us. Two aspects are particularly relevant. The first is that Jesus knew what it was to have to 'function' within the constraints and potential pressures of the clock. Although, as we shall be seeing, He was not actually controlled by time, He was aware of our own significant restrictions in that area. He was 'touched with the feeling of our infirmities' (Hebrews 4:15, KJV). Secondly, Jesus knew that there was a 'timetable' in which He was working. Indeed His Father in heaven had, and continues to have, a timetable in terms of events in this world. It means that we should not fear that God, as we may describe it, is haphazard, unprepared, organising things 'on the hoof', or is caught out and needing to implement 'Plan B'. The Bible declares that God is sovereign in all things. This includes, in ways we cannot understand, the timings of events and specific intervention.

Jesus was aware of time

It was this 'timetable' aspect in respect of Jesus revealing His deity through miraculous intervention that was the issue in this wedding scenario. Mary, Jesus' mother, had no doubt as to the identity of her son. But hardly anyone else was aware of the fact that Jesus was God. Performing a miracle would certainly make people sit up and think. It would raise His 'profile' (a very twenty-first-century concept), getting Him 'noticed'. His 'CV' would also be enhanced. The news of a miracle would, no doubt, have gone viral on social media if the latter had been invented at that time!

SECRECY

However, Jesus was only concerned with doing the will of His Father, and not with taking steps which might be judged appropriate by those around Him. So, in response to His mother's comment, He simply stated that the hour had not yet come for Him to show by means of a miracle to a wider audience that He was God. This was not to be the only occasion. Jesus' earthly (step)brothers were recorded as urging Him to go up to Jerusalem in order to celebrate the Feast of Tabernacles. But He turned down their suggestion to be 'seen': 'I am not going up to this festival, because my time has not yet fully come' (John 7:8). He did subsequently go up to the Feast. However, it is specifically recorded that He went, 'not publicly, but in secret' (John 7:10).

That same secrecy surrounded this first miracle. Jesus actually did intervene regarding the lack of wine following His mother's request. But only a few outsiders knew that there had been a miracle of water being turned to wine. They were the servants who were directed by Jesus to fill six nearby water jars normally used for ceremonial washing. Each of them held between 80 and 100 litres. He then instructed them to draw out the contents and present them to the master of the banquet. The contents now had a very different quality from that of the liquid initially poured into the jars! The master of the banquet was specifically drawn to comment: 'Everyone brings out the choice wine first and then the cheaper wine after the guests have had too much to drink; but you have saved the best till now' (John 2:10). Whether those servants understood the significance of what they witnessed is not stated. However, it is recorded that the disciples, at least, had seen what Jesus had done, both in terms of the quality and quantity. 'He revealed his glory; and his disciples believed in him' (John 2:11).

... adhere to the timing ... His Father had set

The time for Jesus to fully reveal His identity as the Son of God to the world at large by means of miraculous signs had not yet arrived. He knew that He needed to adhere to the timing that His Father had set, and not do what others might expect or prematurely reveal. Nonetheless Jesus was prepared to perform a miracle, albeit privately, out of compassion, while keeping to the overall purposes of God. In due course He would incontrovertibly disclose to all those around that He was the Son of God, thereby setting in motion the series of events that would eventually lead Him to the cross.

24

WHEN, NOT IF

Timing can be a crucial element with regard to decisions that we might have to make. It can arise in particularly big choices such as those I faced in respect of my employment. God has a timetable that is applicable for every situation. Having been in the lower echelons of the civil service, undertaking a number of roles for much of my working life, I was facing the particular prospect of leaving and qualifying for a payoff. Since the civil service provided for this to be awarded within a broad age range, it was not a straightforward choice. However, because of the changing nature and style of management within the department where I worked, it was more a case of 'when' and not 'if' I chose to leave. But I was also aware of the need to listen to what God was saying about the 'when' aspect, especially as the financial implications in this scenario could be far-reaching. The length of time that I remained in the civil service would be reflected in the size of that financial settlement.

The crucial factor in terms of schedule arose when yet another reorganisation in the office was planned. I had been involved in a small project for some months which was now drawing to a close. There were indications that I would be steered, with others, into a very different area of work. For several reasons I was not happy with this prospect and felt, in continuing to pray about the situation, that this was the signal from God to make that decision about leaving. My resignation letter was consequently pulled out, signed and dated! It was a big (and scary!) step to take, but subsequent events, unseen at the time, indicated that it was correct, especially in terms of the timing.

We may not find it easy to discern God's timing in respect of action that we need to take, but He is able and willing to show it to us if we ask. The psalmist brings reassurance concerning issues connected to time: 'The Lᴏʀᴅ makes firm the steps of the one who delights in him ['The steps of a good man are ordered by the Lᴏʀᴅ', KJV]' (Psalm 37:23).

* * *

REFLECTION

Grounds for hope (as seen in this chapter):

- Jesus' miracles were a sign that He was God – we are followers of the miracle-performing Jesus!
- Jesus was living His life with regard to the perfect timetable set by His Father in heaven.
- His timing with regard to performing miracles did not always match the expectations of other people but worked for the best.

POINTS TO PONDER

1. How often are you aware of time and its constraints/ pressures? Tick as many boxes as apply.

Always ☐
Often ☐
Regularly ☐
Infrequently ☐
Never ☐

2. How reassuring do you find it, knowing that God is aware of the pressures that we experience on account of time?

3. How does it affect your relationship with God to know that He has plans for this world in which timing is an essential element, and also plans for your life which also involve timing?

4. In what areas of your life are you particularly needing to be sensitive to God's timing as to when things should be done?

5. In what ways can a close and deepening relationship with God be important in having awareness regarding His timing?

4

AHEAD OF TIME

Then the father realised that this was the exact time at which Jesus had said to him, 'Your son will live.' So he and his whole household believed.

(John 4:53)

Read: John 4:43–54

'What God hath wrought' was the first message of the internet age... back in 1844! Of course the internet itself didn't get operational until a bit later, in November 1990. That was when computers were linked on a global basis and triggered a communications revolution that we now take for granted. Although this network was based on previous work undertaken by the US military, initially in the 1960s, it was the work of an American a hundred years earlier that had made this feasible. Samuel Morse invented the hardware by which messages could be almost instantly communicated by electronic means alone. He even introduced a 'binary' code to transmit that first message. 'Dots' and 'dashes' enabled the words of an Old Testament verse (Numbers 23:23), as above, to be sent from Washington to Baltimore. Quite what Samuel Morse's reaction would be if he were to see the development of the internet by way of a smartphone in operation is open to conjecture. The first iPhone was unveiled in 2007 and set the standard for instant communications and information technology which, again, we now accept as commonplace.

THE 'WOW' FACTOR

The sense of wonder at these advances in technology and communications has been quickly lost. Our 'wow' response has limited staying power. Perhaps the initial readers of the Gospel written by John were different from us in that respect. John probably hoped it would be the case because his aim was to feed into that 'wow' factor. This was the reason for him picking out seven miracles of Jesus which particularly revealed His deity. Each one was a distinct pointer to this revelation, as John underlined when he concluded the account of the next one: 'This was the second sign Jesus performed after coming from Judea to Galilee' (John 4:54).

DELAYED RETURN

Integral to this second miracle of Jesus, as it was in the first, was the 'time' element. In fact the time aspect was introduced in the introductory verse: 'After the two days he [Jesus] left for Galilee' (John 4:43). Samaria had been the place of Jesus' departure, after he had deliberately travelled there in order to meet a particular

Samaritan woman at a well where she had gone to draw water (see John 4:1–26). That meeting and subsequent conversation had taken place at midday – not the normal time to undertake water-carrying tasks. The woman's intention, it seemed, had been specifically to avoid other people by going to the well in the heat of the day. But her subsequent encounter with Jesus had resulted in this messed-up woman coming to faith and telling everyone about it!

There was an amazed and positive response from those in the locality to this woman's account regarding Jesus. 'Many of the Samaritans from that town believed in him because of the woman's testimony, "He told me everything I've ever done."' Consequently they 'urged him to stay with them, and he stayed two days' (John 4:39, 40). As a result even more people became believers in Jesus. The Gospel writer makes it quite clear as to their view of Jesus: 'We know that this man really is the Saviour of the world' (John 4:42).

But this delay in leaving Samaria was to have a knock-on effect. When Jesus eventually resumed His journey and returned to Cana in Galilee, there was someone for whom time was a vital feature in his situation. John's account introduces this person as 'a certain royal official' (4:46). Like that woman in Samaria, he was probably on the fringes of his community. It's reckoned that in his position as a royal official he was working in the court of the Roman tetrarch, Herod Antipas. This meant that he was essentially in collusion with the repressive Roman occupation and therefore not necessarily very popular. (Herod was himself responsible for having John the Baptist beheaded.) But it was the official's family situation where the 'time' element was so important. The account states that he had a son who 'lay ill at Capernaum [and] was close to death' (John 4:46–47). Those

... time was a vital feature

further two days' delay in Jesus' return (and the news of it reaching this father) meant that the official had an even clearer picture of his son's deteriorating condition. Time was shaping this situation, and time was running out fast.

URGENCY

It's worth noting that this court official had to make a significant journey, presumably on foot, in order to approach Jesus for help regarding his son. He had to travel from Capernaum to Cana, a distance of around 16 miles. This probably took a day to complete. At the time that he'd left home, his son was 'close to death ['at the point of death', KJV]' (John 4:47). In the father's mind there was almost certainly great fear and turmoil in that the time lapse between his departure and return – aiming to bring Jesus with him – could prove too long. It was this factor that, no doubt, gave rise to the urgency in his approach. He 'begged' Jesus to 'come and heal' his son: 'Sir, come down before my child dies' (4:47, 49, emphasis mine). The man knew that time was out of his hands and that only Jesus could intervene... if He got to his son before it was too late.

AGENDA

However, that was the official's problem. He had an agenda for how things should be resolved, based on the clock. Understandably, perhaps, he saw that the healing of his sick son was to be achieved by Jesus actually coming to Capernaum and to his son's side. But Jesus had a different agenda, a different plan of intervention into this desperate situation, and one that involved a different timescale. Our way of thinking is likely to be similar to the official's. We have the tendency to come to God with our problems, and then presume to tell Him the way in which we want Him to work them out!

There certainly exists in Scripture the encouragement to bring our circumstances to God so that we can experience His intervention. This is advocated by the writer to the Hebrews: 'Let us then approach the throne of grace with confidence, so that we may receive mercy and find grace to help us in our time of need' (Hebrews 4:16). God may, indeed, intervene in ways which we recognise and about which we may have been given insight. But that is not always going to be the case. God may choose to act in ways, and in a timescale, that is different from our own agenda. That was to prove the case in this second miracle.

AUTHORITY OF JESUS...

Jesus' response to the court official demonstrated in an amazing way the authority that He held. In response to the father's repeated plea, we read: '"Go," Jesus replied, "your son will live" ["thy son liveth", KJV]' (John 4:50). Those five words (in the English translation) totally transformed the situation. Jesus' (few) words had power to bring healing to the man's son immediately, even at a distance of several miles. He did not have to be present, in the near proximity of the sick child, in order to bring healing.

...AND HIS TIMING

But there was also the 'time' element. 'Your son will live' indicated that at that very moment in time there was divine power bringing a restoration of health and life. The father would not have to wait for any period of time. There was to be no time-lapse. Jesus' words, similar to our modern communications (when they work), would not suffer any delay in transmission or reception, but be instant in their effect.

This was subsequently verified when the father was still on his way home. The Gospel writer did not want his readers to be left in any doubt as to the divine authority of Jesus in bringing this healing. John records that the father met his servants who were on their way to him with the news that his son was alive. 'When he [the father] enquired as to the time when his son got better, they said to him, "Yesterday, at one in the afternoon, the fever left him"' (John 4:52). It was this information regarding the timing that particularly struck the father. 'Then the father realised that this was the exact time at which Jesus had said to him, "Your son will live"' (John 4:53).

There was to be no time-lapse

As a consequence of this realisation about the specific timing, there came a spiritual change to follow the physical healing: 'So he and his whole household believed.' Perhaps the father had already picked up something that alerted him to an impending miracle in a way that was not on his agenda. Jesus had previously made a seemingly unrelated comment in reply to the man's initial approach: '"Unless you people see signs and wonders," Jesus told him, "you will never believe"' (John 4:48). The official had certainly responded in a positive way to Jesus' subsequent declaration about healing taking place. 'The man took Jesus at his word [that his son would live] and departed' (John 4:50). The intervention of Jesus to effect this miracle would only be actually seen by him in the future, although very soon. But the man believed that this was going to be the case. He would have confirmation, in due time, that Jesus had healed his son.

READY

A similar principle of God working ahead of time is seen in the life of Abraham, the Old Testament patriarch. He had been instructed by God to sacrifice his son, Isaac. On the way to the place of sacrifice, in answer to Isaac's question about the missing sacrificial animal, he stated that 'God himself will provide the lamb for the burnt offering' (Genesis 22:8). Abraham bound Isaac on the altar and raised his knife, but when the Angel of the Lord called from heaven for him not to administer the fatal strike, the father looked up. Being prevented in the nick of time from sacrificing his son, Abraham then saw a ram caught by its horns in a thicket. God knew the need for a sacrifice and worked so that, at the time it was needed, the ram was already trapped, available for that purpose. Abraham's response was to call that place 'The Lord Will Provide ['Jehovahjireh', KJV]' (Genesis 22:14).

ALREADY PROVIDED

Our experience of God working, unseen by us, so that things are sorted out ahead of time may not be at the same life-or-death levels as in the above accounts, but it can still surprise us. It's only recently that I began working on material that, it was suggested, might be suitable for publishing in book form. This was an entirely new and uncharted world to me! But having approached recognised publishers with my material, and been rejected, I realised that I'd have to consider another route. The alternative option was to 'self' ('independently') publish – and there were loads of internet sites offering such services! I found one, already used by someone I knew, that looked suitable and was ready to make contact.

But just before that happened an email dropped into my inbox from a friend. It was actually about an entirely different matter, making an arrangement to meet. However, he mentioned – it seemed almost as an afterthought – the details of someone he knew who had just set up his own self-publishing service. This new business, aimed for Christian writers, was recommended by my friend. I felt strongly that this was something God had sorted out, working ahead of time before I knew anything about 'self-publishing'! The timing (through that email) was a big factor in believing that this situation was God-orchestrated. My subsequent contact with this publisher was the beginning of a beneficial and productive relationship.

* * *

REFLECTION

Grounds for hope (as seen in this chapter):

- The court official had his own agenda regarding how Jesus should resolve his situation but Jesus wasn't restricted by it.
- The official could come to Jesus with his desperate request.
- Jesus spoke words that brought healing even though there was no evidence that they were effective (as the official's sick son was miles away).
- Those words of Jesus brought immediate change even though there was a delay in time before this was confirmed.

POINTS TO PONDER

1. To what extent does the 'time' factor affect your life and planning? What do your answers indicate about the affect that 'time' has on your life and planning? Tick as many boxes as apply.

   In everything that I do ☐
   Only when other people make me aware of it ☐
   Occasionally, irrespective of individual situations ☐
   Only in particular situations where it's necessary ☐
   I'm oblivious to time whatever the situation ☐

2. Why do we have the tendency to pray to God about situations that concern us with a hidden (or not so hidden) agenda regarding how God should resolve things, including the 'time' element?

3. Why do we often find it difficult to trust in what God says (such as in the many promises that He makes in the Bible) before the time arrives when we see something actually happen?

4. What steps can we take to help us trust God to a greater extent before the time comes when we receive an answer from Him?

5. In what situation do you need to trust in the promises of God even though you have not, as yet, seen anything happen in answer to prayer?

5

NOT TOO LATE?

Jesus saw him lying there and learned that he had been in this condition for a long time ...

(John 5:6)

Read: John 5:1–15

'Have I left it too late?' is a question that's probably gone through your mind more than once. Whether this relates to booking a hotel room, visiting someone before they move, or putting a bid on eBay, the sense that no time is now left can be a big pressure. 'Deadlines' may form part of this equation, although why that particular term is used doesn't always make sense (to me, anyway). Sometimes these can be arbitrary, while on other occasions they are set in stone. But whatever the scenario, the linking of 'time' and 'too late' can result in the dreadful realisation that nothing can now be done. Going backwards in time is not possible, the past cannot be changed, and the outcome of being too late has to be faced.

MANY TIMES

A disabled man, the focus of John's narrative (John 5), knew all about being too late. He had probably experienced it many times. Each occasion probably deepened his sense of anguish. By the time John brought him into his Gospel narrative, the man had seemingly given up on himself. Certainly everyone else had given up on him. His reply to Jesus' question as the account proceeded had started off with the words, 'I have no one to help me ...' (John 5:7).

In fact the entire scenario into which Jesus had walked on that occasion was one of despair. He had gone to Jerusalem for a feast of the Jews. The identity of that feast is not disclosed. But what was clearly described was the place where Jesus ended up. This was a pool near the Sheep Gate on the city wall. It had a name, Bethesda, and was surrounded by five covered colonnades. The pool could more appropriately be described as a reservoir. But what marked it out was its use. John stated in stark terms: 'Here a great number of disabled people used to lie – the blind, the lame, the paralysed' (John 5:3).

The reason for such people spending their time in that location was on account of supernatural activity. An angel of the Lord would come 'from time to time' (presumably without any kind of forewarning) and stir up the waters, with the result that whoever was first to step down into those waters would be cured (John 5:4). Scholars are uncertain as to whether this information formed part of John's original Gospel document as these details were only shown in less important manuscripts. However, there must have been a reason for all of these people gathering round the pool, and the disabled man himself implies, in his reply to Jesus, that this occurrence took place regularly.

RAVAGES OF TIME

But the fact that Jesus had approached this man is important in the context of time. One particular detail is recorded about him: he 'had been an invalid for thirty-eight years' (John 5:5). He was lying in an environment of disease and sickness. The ravages of time, bringing decay, degeneration, deterioration, neglect and vulnerability, would no doubt have added to the general atmosphere of hopelessness and despair. On account of modern medical science and social care, we may not experience the effects of ill health in the same way. But the ravages of time can still grip us. This could apply in terms of many issues such as emotional stress, loneliness, unemployment, accommodation problems and financial resources. The man by the Pool of Bethesda had been in his condition for 'a long time', something that John emphasised (5:6).

WORSE-CASE SCENARIO?

However, there was another point that John wanted to underline. The man had not called for Jesus to come to him. It was Jesus who initially saw the man lying there and specifically 'learned that he had been in this condition for a long time' (John 5:6). It was not clear by what means Jesus actually obtained this information. Someone may have told Him, or it may have been specifically revealed to Him by His Father. But it seems that Jesus wanted to find the person who had been an invalid for the longest period of time. He was looking for the 'worse-case scenario'. Among all that 'great number' of disabled people, Jesus deliberately sought out this man.

When Jesus then went up to the man His first action was simply to ask a question: 'Do you want to get well? ['Wilt thou be made whole?' KJV]' (John 5:6). This may have appeared a pointless thing to ask. But it drew out the sense of helplessness and hopelessness that compounded the man's physical condition. Focusing on the only means that he knew by which healing could come – being the first to step into the waters of the pool after they had been stirred up – he replied by describing the help needed to achieve it. But no help came... everyone had given up on him and he had seen no other option that might bring change. Someone else always got ahead of him. Time had taken its toll on him and it was now too late for any possibility of things being different.

LIFE PASSED THEM BY

If this man by the Pool of Bethesda had sensed that life had passed him by and that there was now no hope of anything being any different, he was not alone. Abraham and Sarah were childless and well advanced in age. Sarah had 'borne him no children' (Genesis 16:1) and Abraham was described as being 'as good as dead' in terms of being a father (see Hebrews 11:11). But God came to them, even though it was biologically 'too late' for anything to happen, with the promise that they would become parents. This subsequently happened, Sarah giving birth to Isaac (see Genesis 21:1–7) through God's intervention. A similar situation was faced by the priest Zechariah and Elizabeth his wife in New Testament times. She was 'not able to conceive, and they were both very old' (Luke 1:7). God sent the angel Gabriel to Zechariah to give him the news that he and his wife would become parents to a son to whom they were to give the name John. Their son would prepare the way for Jesus, the Messiah. Zechariah's response of sheer disbelief about this information underlined his mindset that time had passed and it was too late for anything to happen. But it did happen! God enabled Elizabeth to become pregnant and then to give birth as foretold (see Luke 1:57).

... it was biologically 'too late'

Back in the Old Testament again, Moses was someone else who had given up hope on anything being different. Although raised as a prince of Egypt he'd had to flee the country on account of committing murder. For 40 years he had lived out in the wilderness looking after sheep. He was 80 years old when God met him, speaking out of a burning bush. Moses, somewhat like Zechariah, was in disbelief at the prospect of God's intervention to bring change. He baulked at God's call for him, someone now in obscurity and disgrace, to lead his fellow Hebrews out of Egyptian slavery to their Promised Land. He ended up asking God to send, not him, but someone else. But Moses wasn't too old and the situation not 'too late' for God to use him in this role (see Exodus 3:13–17).

So when Jesus came up to this invalid, it seemed that the intention was to heal him, whatever he might say in reply to Jesus' question 'Do you want to get well?' Although his response had been just to describe his helplessness, he did take positive action upon hearing the words of command that Jesus then spoke: 'Get up! Pick up your mat and walk' (John 5:8). The healing that Jesus brought was instantaneous: 'At once the man was cured; he picked up his mat and walked' (5:9).

NEVER TOO LATE

There is an important factor to be seen in this account in respect of time. The man had indirectly referred to time in his reply to Jesus – someone else got to the waters of the pool in a quicker time than himself. However, Jesus' words of command and the consequent healing showed something else: with God it's never too late.

Not only had this been evident in the situations previously described in relation to Abraham and Sarah, Moses, and Zechariah and Elizabeth, but it was shown in other miraculous healings. These included the woman who had been suffering from bleeding for 12 years, and another woman bowed over with a back condition for 18 years (see, respectively, Luke 8:43–44; 13:10–13). Both scenarios suggested that it was now too late for anything to change.

It seems that our own age also has its agendas and expectations regarding when things should (or should not) happen, the stages at which certain 'life events' should occur. If those events have not happened, then the possibility of any change is written off. Sadly this kind of mindset is often accepted by Christians in general as well as church leaders. We get sucked into accepting certain timescales in regard, for example, to education, relationships, raising a family, work experience or changing careers. But with God it's never too late. I have one friend who found that to be true – getting married at age 68; another married in his late fifties and is now the proud father of three children. A friend's mother qualified for her pilot's licence at age 78, studied to earn a degree at age 84, and got a book published at age 89!

... our own age also has its agendas

JUST A FEW MOMENTS

The disabled man's healing was specifically brought by Jesus speaking those words of command. This showed a second major factor with regard to God working in the dimension of time. The man by the pool had been an invalid for years. He had, we may presume, woken up that morning probably like every other morning for a very long time. There was not the remotest suggestion that the day ahead would be any different from those before it. Even when Jesus approached him, there was no indication that anything significant was about to take place. But when Jesus spoke those few words, divine power was released... and immediately there was a change. God can bring, even following years of 'nothingness', total and complete change in just a few moments.

Again this is not an isolated example. The Gospels record that people's lives and circumstances were changed simply by Jesus speaking. 'Be clean', 'Come out of this man', 'Stretch out your hand', 'Receive your sight', 'My child, get up', 'Lazarus, come out', 'Quiet! Be still', 'Go, show yourselves to the priests'. These few words were spoken, respectively, to a leper (Mark 1:41), a demonised man (Mark 5:8), a man with a withered arm (Mark 3:5), a blind man (Luke 18:42), Jairus' daughter (Luke 8:54), Lazarus (John 11:43), a fierce storm (Mark 4:39) and ten lepers (Luke 17:14).

Those interventions of Jesus by speaking with authority and power brought healing, life and change to those who were afflicted – and all in a moment of time. They showed that time-lapses of long duration do not always have to be worked through when we experience God's intervention. John's record of the invalid's healing did not miss out that aspect: 'At once the man was cured ...' (John 5:9). This immediacy of events only features in John's record on a few other occasions: 'immediately' (John 6:21); 'at that moment' (John 18:27).

THE WRONG DAY?

However, there was a further aspect of time which related to this miracle. There is almost a sense of foreboding as John then records in his account, 'The day on which this took place was a Sabbath' (John 5:9). This seemed to inexorably lead to a confrontation: '... and so the Jews said to the man who had been healed, "It is the Sabbath; the law forbids you to carry your mat"' (John 5:10). The Jewish religious leaders wanted to put time constraints on what God could or could not do. As evidenced on other occasions, there was ongoing conflict between their restrictive interpretation of the Law on Sabbath activity, and Jesus' view. This reached a climax when, on another occasion, Jesus answered those critics by accusing them of being 'hypocrites!' They would perform actions of untying and leading their livestock to water on the Sabbath, so why should someone not be set free from satanic binding? (See the case of the crippled woman; Luke 13:15–16.)

God chose the time for releasing the disabled man from his longstanding illness, even though others, on account of tradition and religiosity, considered it the 'wrong day'. Jesus was aware of timing in respect of His work on this earth. He subsequently stated: 'My Father is always at his work to this very day, and I too am working'; 'As long as it is day, we must do the works of him who sent me. Night is coming, when no one can work' (John 5:17; 9:4). The Gospel accounts record the different times when Jesus was doing this work of Him who sent Him. This included the night hours, early morning, midday, evening and late afternoon. As Jesus showed, God doesn't work according to our limitations or expectations, which might involve coffee breaks, holidays, 'time out', gap years, sabbaticals or retirement (to name just a few). This means that not only can we come to God at any point during the day or night, and on any day of the week (not just Sunday when at church), but we can experience His work in our lives at any time. This even includes Monday morning at work!

LATER...

But there is one last point in respect of time that John includes in this account. It is prefaced by the word 'Later' (John 5:15). Jesus subsequently found the man who'd been healed, when he was in the temple. The man had already exchanged comments with the Jews about his experience. Now Jesus met him again. On this occasion a warning was brought: 'See, you are well again. Stop sinning or something worse may happen to you' (John 5:14). The original Greek for the phrase 'Stop sinning' is in the present tense and so could be read, 'No longer continue to sin.' Jesus knew that this man needed to have a right relationship with God, without which his spiritual condition would be even worse than his longstanding physical disability. Jesus was not only aware of the man's past situation, but He also knew of the future possibility. He knows the same about us. Our perspective on time needs adjusting to God's perspective, realising the impact of present behaviour on the future that lies ahead. For the moment we are in a time when, with God, it's not too late, whether in terms of our physical afflictions or spiritual state. 'Now is the time of God's favour, now is the day of salvation' (2 Corinthians 6:2). Are we living our lives in the light of it?

* * *

REFLECTION

Grounds for hope (as seen in this chapter):

- Jesus is aware of situations in which a long period of time has elapsed without any change being experienced.
- Even though we (or others) may have given up on situations ever changing, Jesus never gives up on us.
- With Jesus it's never too late for Him to intervene and bring change.

POINTS TO PONDER

1. What are the effects of feeling that time has passed us by and that it's now too late for anything to change? Tick as many boxes as apply.

   Other people give up on us ☐

   We give up on ourselves ☐

   We see no future prospects ☐

   Past experience provides no basis of hope ☐

   We feel that God has forgotten us ☐

2. This account in John 5 indicates that Jesus was specifically looking out for the worse-case scenario – the person who had been sick the longest. Why is it important to note that this was not an isolated example (see Luke 8:43; Luke 13:11; John 9:1)?

3. Why do you think it's important to know that Jesus never gives up on us even though, on account of time passing by, others may have done so?

4. Why do you feel it's important to know that Jesus can bring change even when situations seem to be too late for anything to happen?

5. In what situation do you need to experience Jesus as one for whom it's never too late?

6

COUNTDOWN
TO CHAOS

When Jesus looked up and saw a great crowd coming towards him, he
said to Phillip, 'Where shall we buy bread for these people to eat?'
(John 6:5)

Read: John 6:1–15

There are occasions when we hit problems that seem to come out of the blue, appearing unexpectedly. Driving, as I do, a classic car, this is not an unknown experience. Although the Morris 1000 is the quintessential British car, known for being reliable and robust, its vintage has to be taken into account. Mechanical bits of the vehicle can give out without notice. So, travelling on one occasion down to the West Country (of England), everything was running smoothly and then, suddenly, there was a loud bang. This was accompanied by a cloud of steam rising from the engine and the car stopping dead. The water pump had failed, causing the engine to overheat and seize up. The worn-out pump was eventually and easily replaced – by a garage mechanic, not me! But this was a problem that could not have been foreseen, especially as my vehicle had only basic monitoring that did not include an engine temperature gauge.

However, other problems can be seen looming on the horizon, ready to impact us if no avoidance action is taken. It's those difficulties which can come into the category of a 'countdown' to chaos. Unless something is done in the time that remains, trouble will ensue. The workplace is a breeding ground for this kind of event. My experience from within a government department has been typical of many office situations. The small team of which I was a member at one stage was understaffed and unable to cope with the volume of cases we were needing to handle. More and more time was being spent answering phone and email enquiries about the backlog than actually working to reduce it. This was a recipe for trouble. Despite regular statistical returns and emails pointing out the situation to the higher echelons of management, nothing was done. It was only when questions were asked at a senior level that steps were taken, staff were allocated to help us, and meltdown was avoided.

THE TICKING CLOCK

There are, however, even more important issues in life where a countdown seems to be pointing to only one result as time moves on. Deteriorating physical or mental health, a failing business, a church with a shrinking number of committed members, a looming court case, an inevitable phone call or email… these can all signal an end coming into sight. The clock is ticking, the days on the calendar are being crossed off, the countdown is in full swing.

This may have been the feeling that the disciples of Jesus were experiencing in the hours leading up to the most amazing miracle that they witnessed prior to Jesus being raised from the dead. The impact of this miracle, the feeding of the five thousand, was so massive that it was recorded by all four Gospel writers. Apart from the actual resurrection of Jesus it was the only one that they all picked up. John, it seems, was particularly careful about the miracles that he included in his Gospel. Each of the seven that was featured was selected because it emphasised the divinity of Christ. These accounts were a 'sign' pointing to His power as the Son of God. The only other miracle that he records that is found elsewhere is Jesus walking on water. So this narrative of feeding the vast crowd was clearly an impressive intervention of God that John recognised as needing to be incorporated into his collection.

PRE-LAUNCH FOREBODING

The day of that miracle had not started by indicating any countdown coming into operation. Matthew's description of events opens with Jesus receiving news of John the Baptist's death. The latter had been beheaded on the callous orders of Herod Antipas who was ruler over part of Palestine. Jesus' response to this tragic event was to withdraw 'by boat privately to a solitary place' (Matthew 14:13). Mark and Luke, in their accounts, although mentioning John the Baptist's execution, indicate a further reason for leaving the immediate area. Mark quotes Jesus as instructing his disciples, 'Come with me by yourselves to a quiet place and get some rest' (Mark 6:31). This was in response to the disciples reporting back on their mission trip and, as evidenced from Jesus' comment, needing 'time out'

The countdown to chaos started ticking

because of all the people around them preventing them from even having the chance to eat.

However, the plans to 'get away from it all' did not materialise. The countdown to chaos started ticking when the crowd recognised Jesus, noticing that He was leaving the area. They consequently followed Him. Matthew's account records that Jesus and His disciples had withdrawn by boat. Luke adds that they landed across the Sea of Galilee at a town called Bethsaida (Luke 9:11). John's account comes alongside these others at this point, confirming the journey to the 'far shore', adding that this all took place near the time of the Jewish Passover festival (John 6:1, 4).

EMERGING PROBLEM

It was that crowd element that precipitated the emerging problem. While Jesus and the disciples had sailed (or rowed) across the water, the people had run 'on foot from all the towns and villages' and arrived ahead of them (as recorded in Mark 6:33). Matthew, Mark and Luke each give details of Jesus' response to seeing all these people. Even though it was not on the 'agenda', He 'healed those who were ill' (Matthew 14:14); 'began teaching them many things' (Mark 6:34); 'welcomed them and spoke to them about the kingdom of God' (Luke 9:11). Matthew and Mark both state the reason for Jesus' response: it arose from His compassion 'because they were like sheep without a shepherd'.

While John's account is silent about those actions of Jesus in healing and teaching, he is almost abrupt in raising the problem that was looming ahead. 'Jesus', he records, 'looked up and saw

54

a great crowd coming towards him.' Jesus
then asked Philip, 'Where shall we buy   ... the time
bread for these people to eat?' But the   on the clock
other Gospel writers are also aware of
this problem. Each makes a clear
reference to the time on the clock. 'As evening approached ...'
(Matthew 14:15); 'By this time it was late in the day ...' (Mark
6:35); 'Late in the afternoon ...' (Luke 9:12).

Whether Jesus was aware of time moving on is not recorded.
John subsequently records, 'he already had in mind what he was
going to do' (John 6:6), which indicates that Jesus knew that time
was passing but was not troubled by it. For Him there was no
countdown to chaos, but a countdown to crumbs being
multiplied.

It can only be conjectured, but it would seem that the disciples
themselves began to be aware of a looming problem. Perhaps
they started to exchange glances as the sun got lower in the sky.
They may have started to calculate the cost of providing food and
where it might be obtained before it got too late. There is also
the possibility that they edged nearer to Jesus in order to check
whether the healing and teaching was likely to be prolonged.

NOT HOLDING BACK

Finally the disciples couldn't hold it back. Matthew records their
words at perhaps the point of no return: 'the disciples came to
Him and said: "This is a remote place, and it's already getting
late. Send the crowds away, so that they can go to the villages and
buy themselves some food"' (Matthew 14:15). Mark adds to that
proposition by stating that the disciples pointed out that it was
'very late' (Mark 6:35). Luke's contribution to the overall picture

is to put into the disciples' mouths the suggestion that not only food was needed by the crowd, but also lodgings. It must have been a noticeably advanced hour for that aspect to have been brought into the equation (Luke 9:12)!

A THOUSAND PLACES TO SEE?

It's appropriate to pause at this point. The disciples were metaphorically fixing their eyes on the clock. Time was dictating their attitudes and actions. As time was passing, so their anxiety was increasing – in proportion, it may seem, to the countdown getting closer to 'zero'. Their words hinted at urgency and desperation. Action was needed or else there would be real trouble. Hungry and tired people, especially a large group of them, can be difficult to handle; chaos was looming.

In our own age we are particularly confronted with countdowns. Those deadlines, target dates, trigger points, schedules and timelines feature prominently. Perhaps these implicit pressures can be illustrated by the title of the book *1,000 Places to See Before You Die*. It's questionable whether many expectations such as studying at university, buying a house, having a lucrative career, achieving promotion, travelling extensively, visiting those '1000 places', are appropriate objectives to be achieved within a particular timeframe.

The disciples had possibly been working on a 'Plan B'. This emerged when Jesus, in response to their suggestion to send the crowd away, stated: 'They do not need to go away. You give them something to eat' (Matthew 14:16). At that point the disciples answered, seemingly without a pause, 'We have here only five loaves of bread and two fish' (Matthew 14:17). John describes them as 'small barley' loaves and 'small' fish (John 6:9). Although

Mark's account raises possibilities – immediately ruled out of hand – of buying in food supplies, that information regarding food supplies indicates that the disciples had already been checking available resources. Making enquiries among several thousand people regarding the edible contents of their daypacks (or whatever) would have taken time. So the 12 disciples could have been working on such an inventory even as the sun was disappearing over the horizon.

ZERO HOUR

John's account records the details of the actual source of those loaves and fishes. He has also previously put that question into Jesus' mouth to Philip: 'Where shall we buy bread for this people to eat?' The detail is then added: 'He asked this only to test him, for he already had in mind what he was going to do' (John 6:6). That countdown seemed to have got to 'zero hour'. But then, among all that crowd, Andrew had earlier (it seems) found the only available food, owned by a boy. Andrew's summation of the situation probably voiced everyone's thoughts: 'But how far will they go among so many?' (John 6:9). The Gospel writers then describe the ensuing miracle. Jesus, after commanding the people to sit down, 'gave thanks'. Then He broke the loaves, before giving them to His disciples to distribute to the people (although John doesn't explicitly mention the involvement of those disciples in handing out the loaves and fishes). The same process occurred with the fish.

The leftovers after everyone had eaten, consisting of 12 basketfuls, are also recorded in each of the Gospel accounts. John specifically states that the disciples had distributed 'to those who were seated as much [food] as they wanted' (John 6:11). The other accounts describe how everyone had eaten and was 'satisfied'.

OLD TESTAMENT

The miracle of the feeding of the five thousand was not entirely unique. The Old Testament prophets Elijah and Elisha each experienced God's intervention in multiplying food resources in order to provide for those in need. In Elijah's case it was a small quantity of flour and oil, possessed by a widow at a place called Zarephath, being used to feed her, her son and the prophet for an undisclosed period (1 Kings 17:7–16). Elisha spoke God's word over a small supply of barley loaves so that a hundred men were fed (2 Kings 4:42–44). However, the feeding of five thousand was not only a miracle of mega proportions, but was enacted against this particular backdrop of time.

THE TIME FACTOR

Time had clearly been the big factor for the disciples. But it was not on Jesus' agenda. His priority was in bringing healing and teaching to the people, showing them the kingdom of God. He didn't have to be concerned about the clock because 'he already had in mind what he was going to do'.

In a way that we cannot understand, Jesus also knows what is ahead of us and what future days hold in store. It means that any 'countdown' scenario is not to dominate our perspective. Jesus can be trusted with regard to situations that may, to us, look like heading towards chaos. This may involve His miraculous intervention, as we may view it. But it may also involve us being like Andrew, the disciple, and working out what resources or opportunities we already possess, however unhelpful they may seem.

58

OMINOUS COUNTDOWN

The unlikely setting of a submarine in World War Two involved some of these factors... alongside an ominous countdown. This featured HMS Seal of the British navy which was operating underwater in hostile seas. It hit a mine which exploded, causing damage to the stern of the vessel, resulting in it being weighed down and embedded on the ocean floor. The submarine captain, Lieutenant Commander Rupert Lonsdale, ordered the ballast tanks to be blown but this had no effect. The submarine was trapped on the sea floor, having already been submerged for many hours. The clock was ticking, air was running out, and the crew were in serious trouble. The inevitable outcome seemed only a short period of time ahead.

There seemed to be no escape. But Commander Lonsdale was a committed Christian and believed in the Bible, especially the verse, 'All things are possible with God' (see Matthew 19:26). So he turned to his crew and prayed aloud for God's help. He then invited his men to join him in saying the Lord's Prayer. The answer to their prayers came almost immediately and actually lay within their power. Lonsdale suddenly had an idea (no doubt given by God) which involved rigging a rope the entire length of the submarine on which crew members were instructed to haul themselves to the top of the tilting vessel. Then, using this human ballast and ordering for the remaining compressed air tanks to be blown, the engines were run at full power. With agonising slowness the rear broke free from the mud on the seabed and the submarine rose to the surface, and safety. Again, it was shown that no countdown is outside God's control or ability to miraculously intervene.

* * *

REFLECTION

Grounds for hope (as seen in this chapter):

- Jesus was aware of time passing by, but was not troubled by it.
- Jesus knew, in advance, 'what he was going to do' even though there was no obvious solution to the looming problem.
- Even when 'zero hour' was reached, Jesus was in control of the situation.

POINTS TO PONDER

1. What are the effects of feeling that time is passing (as, perhaps, shown by the disciples) with no obvious solution, and that we are on a 'countdown to chaos'? What do your answers indicate about the way you might react to impending trouble? Tick as many boxes as apply.

We focus entirely on the looming problem ☐
We work on 'Plan B' ☐
We keep looking at our watch or calendar ☐
We hope that God gets through His agenda quickly ☐
We get totally locked into worry and anxiety ☐

2. What other accounts in Jesus' ministry involved this element of a situation heading for disaster as the clock kept ticking?

3. Why is it important to realise that Jesus always knows what He is 'going to do' even though we may not see any solution ahead of us?

4. The disciples were aware of the time that Jesus was spending in healing and teaching the people in that crowd arising from His compassion... and aware of that 'countdown'. How should we respond when God is clearly working in a particular way and yet seems oblivious to problems that we can see up ahead?

5. In what situation are you experiencing a 'countdown to chaos' problem that you need to bring and entrust to Jesus?

7

A CHANGED DIMENSION

By now it was dark, and Jesus had not yet joined them.

(John 6:17)

Read: John 6:16–21

Darkness, especially that of night-time, is not just a physical sensation. With greatly diminished or even non-existent vision can also come overwhelming feelings of vulnerability, aloneness and helplessness. We can feel totally out of control. So probably all of us, at least sometimes, avoid pitch-black conditions as much as we can. That's fairly straightforward if you live and work in cities and towns. But out in the countryside it's a different matter. Darkness can be both gripping and penetrating; all the physical senses are desperately probing to find something – anything – with which to 'connect', to avoid total disorientation… and panic!

So, trying to negotiate unlit country roads and lanes in the dark has always been a challenge, sometimes unnerving, in this age of motoring. That's why drivers have reason to thank a man named Percy Shaw. He was the innovator of the 'cat's eyes' – reflecting studs that have been inserted in the middle of the road surface, aiding drivers along perhaps winding and hilly roads in the countryside. It is said that Shaw hit upon the idea when driving along such roads and a cat, sitting at the side of the highway, turned its head into the beam of his headlights as he drove towards it. As to the fate of this animal, history is silent! But the resultant idea of small mirror-type reflecting glass 'eyes', set in small rubber casings that sink into the road when a vehicle drives over them, was a simple but effective solution to this problem. It brought a great increase in the safety factor for motorists driving at night. Although, apparently, the original style of 'cat's eyes' has now been supplanted by LED equivalents, the principle that was patented back in 1934 still helps us deal with the perils of being in the dark.

ON A HIGH

'Darkness' was the dominant feature of Jesus' next miraculous 'sign' recorded by John. Time was integral to this factor, in terms of both the unfolding events and the sequel. These events followed immediately after the miraculous feeding of the five thousand. Perhaps the disciples were on a 'high' at what they had witnessed. This was not only in respect of the vast crowd that had been fed from just five 'small' loaves and two 'small' fishes, but also the fact that the leftovers, when gathered together, filled 12 baskets. Clearly the main miracle had made a huge impact on the people themselves who, consequently, wanted to make Jesus king by force (see John 6:15).

So the disciples, in that sense of wonderment, seemingly made no comment when Jesus, prior to withdrawing to a mountain by Himself, directed them to get into their boat. He told them to head across the Sea of Galilee for Capernaum (John 6:16–17; Mark records that the disciples were to go to 'Bethsaida' [Mark 6:45] but then concludes the account by describing them as landing at 'Gennesaret'). Meanwhile Jesus' purpose in going to the mountain was in order to pray (Matthew 14:23; Mark 6:46). It is John who records the time of day on which the disciples began their voyage: 'When evening came ... By now it was dark' (John 6:16, 17). The disciples didn't question the element of risk in going across the lake – well known for sudden storms – as directed by Jesus. Nor did they seem to notice or raise concerns about the absence of Jesus Himself in undertaking their journey.

POINT OF NO RETURN

Matthew and Mark's accounts pick up the 'time' element as they describe the conditions which the disciples encountered as they attempted to travel across the Sea of Galilee. 'Later that night, he [Jesus] was there alone [on the mountainside], and the boat was already a considerable distance from land, buffeted by the waves because the wind was against it' (Matthew 14:23–24). Mark specifies that as a consequence of these adverse conditions the disciples were 'straining at the oars' (Mark 6:48). John highlights the atrocious weather: 'A strong wind was blowing and the waters grew rough' (John 6:18).

The overall effect of the wind and turbulent sea was that the disciples had rowed only three or three-and-a-half miles across the lake (John 6:19). This would mean that they were about halfway through their voyage. But it had taken them several hours to achieve even that distance. That time estimate is based

... halfway through their voyage

on Matthew and Mark's descriptions of what happened next. 'Shortly before dawn ... ['about the fourth watch of the night ...' KJV]' (Matthew 14:25; Mark 6:48). This period of time was reckoned to be between three and six o'clock in the morning. They were beyond the 'point of no return'. The disciples were in a bad situation with little energy remaining to battle against the elements in order to attempt to reach safety in whatever direction it lay.

TERROR... 'DON'T BE AFRAID'

But it was the actual event that then took place which John, along with the other two Gospel writers (Matthew and Mark), specifically describe: 'they saw Jesus approaching the boat, walking on the water' (John 6:19). Matthew and Mark agree with this amazing scene: 'the disciples saw him walking on the lake' (Matthew 14:26); 'he went out to them, walking on the lake' (Mark 6:48). They also all agree on the reaction of the disciples to this amazing miracle: 'terrified' (Matthew 14:26); 'terrified' (Mark 6:50); 'frightened' (John 6:19). Matthew and Mark record that the disciples thought they were seeing a ghost and cried out in fear. Finally there is also agreement on Jesus' response to His disciples' terror: 'Take courage! It is I. Don't be afraid' (Matthew 14:27; Mark 6:50; John 6:20 – John's narrative omits the 'take courage' element).

Matthew, alone of the Gospel writers, adds the sequel to Jesus' words of reassurance – that Peter also (briefly!) walked on water. Both Matthew and Mark describe Jesus climbing into the boat and how the wind died down.

But John adds a short addendum to his account. This was also a factor that involved time. He states: 'Then they were willing to take him [Jesus] into the boat, and immediately the boat reached the shore where they were heading' (John 6:21).

TIME INTERWOVEN

That last comment by John in his account means that this miracle involved two aspects in which 'time' was interwoven. In the first instance the miracle of Jesus walking on the water took place at night, or at least in the very early hours of the morning. The fact that the clock was recording an early hour did not preclude Jesus from intervening in a miraculous way. We may, perhaps subconsciously, feel that God will only act during the waking hours or is (somehow) prevented from working in the dark. But, as the psalmist stated:

> ... an early hour did not preclude Jesus

> He who watches over you will not slumber;
> indeed, he who watches over Israel
> will neither slumber nor sleep ...

> he will watch over your life;
> the LORD will watch over your coming and going
> both now and for evermore.
> (Psalm 121:4–8)

God works the 'night shift' as well as the 'day shift'.

UNDERGROUND EXPLOSION – 2010

When an underground explosion rocked the mineshaft of some workings in Chile in 2010, it resulted in 33 miners being trapped more than 2,000 feet under the earth's surface. They looked doomed. No contact was possible with the emergency services that had been assembled at ground level. There was no way that they could be told that everyone had actually survived the blast or where they were located within the mine workings. But one of the trapped miners, Jose Henriques, was a Christian and believed that God could save them in answer to prayer. So he got his fellow miners to join him in praying for God to intervene. Meanwhile, on the surface, the rescue services were drilling boreholes down in the general direction of the mine to try and locate any survivors. One of these attempts resulted in the drill hitting a hard rock surface and being diverted... into the precise chamber where the miners were sheltering!

In fact the immediate survival of those miners following the explosion had been a 'miracle' involving time. They had been taking their lunch break in a rest area away from the mine workings when the blast occurred, and were therefore distant from its devastating effects. So no one had actually been injured. Now that the rescuers had located the men it took some time before a larger hole could be bored. This eventually enabled the miners, after 69 days trapped underground, to be brought to the surface, one by one, in a specially constructed capsule. Jose and his companions were in no doubt that God had enabled them to be rescued through the efforts of those on the surface, God working through the night hours (as well as the daytime) for rescue to be accomplished.

IMMEDIATELY

The second of those 'time' elements involved that word 'immediately' used by John in his account. It indicated that there was no time-lapse between Jesus getting into the disciples' boat and everyone arriving at their destination on the shore. It's not clear why, of all the three Gospel writers, John was the only one to describe this situation. The original Greek word translated as 'immediately' meant 'straight away', 'directly', 'suddenly', 'quickly'. Perhaps this was simply the perception of the disciples. They were so amazed at what had taken place that they didn't realise how much time it took to complete their voyage. For them, time might have flown.

But perhaps it reflects a particular intervention by God with regard to time; this is suggested in biblical accounts regarding Elijah in the Old Testament, and Philip in the New Testament. The former, a prophet, was described as having the 'power of the LORD' come upon him, which resulted in him being able to run ahead of the king (Ahab) in his chariot, and consequently arrive first at the destination of Jezreel (see 1 Kings 18:45–46). Elijah covered the distance in a much quicker time than seemed possible.

The 'time' element was even more evident with regard to Philip the Evangelist. As a result of his encounter with an Ethiopian eunuch, the latter requested baptism, which Phillip undertook there in the desert. But as soon as they came out of the water the account states that 'the Spirit of the Lord suddenly took Philip away, and the eunuch did not see him again … Philip, however, appeared at Azotus and travelled about' (Acts 8:39–40). From this description of the situation it seems that Philip was immediately and supernaturally transported, in a moment of time, to a distant location.

FLEXI-TIME

Although not in anything like the same league as these biblical examples, I seem to have experienced some form of God's intervention with regard to time. This was more in terms of it being 'squeezed' rather than God causing events to happen instantaneously. But it was still something that I couldn't really explain. It arose in connection with my church holding regular early morning prayer meetings, facilitated for those like myself who had a job during the day. This meant a change of routine. On the mornings when these meetings were held, I would emerge from my house at some unearthly hour, and point my bicycle up the road (towards the church) instead of down, the normal route to my office. When the meeting was over I would retrace my journey on the bicycle towards London and work.

In theory the resultant late start should have severely impacted my 'flexi-time' record showing my hours in the office. I was careful in accurately documenting my time at work, and stayed only slightly longer (as I judged it) to compensate to some extent for these later arrivals. However, in a way that I could not work out, when reconciling my overall times (for 'flexi-working time' purposes) there was never any significant loss of overall time (or output) arising from this situation. Somehow God seemed to overrule so that my journey back to work from church was not taking as long as I thought, and the additional period at the other 'end' of the day was sufficient to make up any deficit arising from this later start. Perhaps we should not assume that God will always somehow intervene in time in such a way, but it's not outside of His ability to do so.

A little-known verse highlights this aspect of time and God. The Old Testament records that one of the kings of Judah, Hezekiah, took steps to bring the nation back to God. This involved the restoration of temple worship following years of neglect. When this was accomplished it was recorded: 'Hezekiah and all the people rejoiced at what God had brought about for his people, because it was done so quickly' (2 Chronicles 29:36). Our God is One who can 'speed up' time!

* * *

REFLECTION

Grounds for hope (as seen in this chapter):

- The fact that the clock was recording an early hour did not preclude Jesus from working in a miraculous way.
- Jesus knew of the storm that the disciples were encountering during the hours of darkness.
- Jesus was able, in some way, to 'speed up' time.

POINTS TO PONDER

1. Why do we sometimes feel that Jesus only works (or miraculously intervenes) during certain times, and not at others (especially at night)? Tick as many boxes as apply.

   We know that we need time to rest/recover, and assume Jesus also needs it ☐

   We don't sense the presence of Jesus and think that means He's not at work ☐

   We are overwhelmed by the sense of darkness which prevents us from seeing Jesus ☐

   We are preoccupied by trying to deal with the 'storm' and don't think about Jesus ☐

   We think that the miracles of Jesus are now past events and not for us now ☐

2. What steps can we take to help us keep our minds focused on Jesus even when we are experiencing dark and stormy situations?

3. What is the importance of maintaining our trust in Jesus even when time is passing, the storms continue, and there is no indication of His presence or intervention?

4. Why is it necessary for us to take into account that, in some way, Jesus is able to intervene in the passage of time so that, to us, events or circumstances are speeded up?

5. In what situation are you experiencing darkness and storms, with no indication of Jesus being present, in which you need to maintain hope that He will intervene in time?

8

NOT LOOKING BACK

*He replied, 'Whether he is a sinner or not, I don't know. One thing I
do know. I was blind but now I see!'*

(John 9:25)

Read: John 9:1–41

'Retro-styling' impacts even hand luggage! One of my
nephews spotted my designer shoulder bag and commented
on its original 'look'. From its well-used appearance he then
deduced that it was actually an original, not a 'retro'. My attempt
to look vaguely trendy was therefore wasted! But it did illustrate
the way that designers and manufacturers across a whole
spectrum of goods and services have realised the value and
attraction of nostalgia.

The 'past' is a particular necessity in the tourism industry.
London, of course, is full of it. Even mundane-looking buildings

have ended up on the tourist map because of some historic connection associated with people's fame... or ignominy. The latter includes the little-known throat surgeon, Sir Morell Mackenzie. Plaques in Westminster and Leytonstone (east London) mark, respectively, his residence and birthplace. He was responsible for a monumental misdiagnosis of the German Crown Prince's condition, leading to the prince's premature death (as Emperor Frederick III). His successor was the notorious Emperor Kaiser Wilhelm II. But fascination with history has meant such plaques are retained even though they may commemorate someone in the past whose actions had dire consequences.

QUESTIONS ABOUT THE PAST

It was the past that also seemed to grip the disciples of Jesus when, on their travels, they saw a man who was blind. This, sadly, was not an uncommon sight. As subsequently stated (John 9:8), he was begging. But what drew him to the disciples' attention was that the man, now an adult, had actually been born blind many years previously. This raised a question, also relating to the past, which they directed to Jesus: 'Rabbi, who sinned, this man or his parents, that he was born blind?' (John 9:2).

Behind that insensitive question was a particular mindset. The Jewish religious teachers had developed a principle that linked suffering with sin. This held that sickness, a form of suffering, could arise from someone's personal sin or that of their parents. Jeremiah, the Old Testament prophet, had been prompted to refer to the latter idea, declaring that God refuted it:

> In those days people will no longer say, 'The parents have eaten sour grapes, and the children's teeth are set on edge.'

Instead, everyone will die for their own sin; whoever eats sour grapes – their own teeth will be set on edge.

(Jeremiah 31:29–30)

However, that same passage looked ahead to Jesus:

'The days are coming,' declares the LORD ...
'I will put my law in their minds
and write it on their hearts.
I will be their God,
and they will be my people ...
For I will forgive their wickedness
and will remember their sins no more.'

(Jeremiah 31:31, 33–34)

This was pointing out that people could no longer excuse their situations and God's judgement on account of the actions of previous generations, thereby absolving themselves from responsibility.

PERSONAL SIN?

This approach resulted in suffering being considered as due to personal sin. So the disciples of Jesus were asking, in effect: 'Does the fact that this man has been born without vision mean that he sinned even prior to his birth?' This was the 'logical' conclusion that had been reached in such circumstances. However, the apostle Paul subsequently corrected this mistaken logic. He clearly showed that this idea of prenatal sin was wrong when he commented on God's choice of Jacob, from whom the Jewish people would stem: 'Yet, *before* the twins [Jacob and Esau] were born *or* had done anything good or bad …' (Romans 9:11, emphasis mine).

BRINGING CHANGE

Jesus was quick to correct this entire set of thinking regarding this particular man's suffering being due to sin. He stated: 'Neither this man nor his parents sinned.' He then went on to explain: 'But this happened so that the works of God might be displayed in him' (John 9:3). The disciples had been looking back in time to try and understand the man's present circumstances. But this would not actually change his current plight nor make any difference to the future. However, Jesus was looking at the situation with a view to bringing God's power upon the man and changing the outlook ahead. This stance was underlined by Jesus' further statement: 'As long as it is day, we must do the works of him who sent me. Night is coming, when no one can work. While I am in the world, I am the light of the world' (John 9:4–5). Jesus was not prepared to simply assess the man's condition but leave him in his afflicted state. He was also going to act ('work'), so that the man would experience change which would affect his future.

… changing the outlook ahead

FIXATION

The emphasis described at the beginning of this chapter about nostalgia can have another angle. We can be drawn into looking backwards in time in a general sense, which can be helpful if the aim is to learn from it and then press forward. But there can also be a negative effect if taken in a personal way. Continually reflecting on past failures, mistakes, disappointments and lost opportunities – in addition to sin which may be part of those experiences – can seriously influence our relationship with God. This, in turn, can affect the plans that He has for us concerning the future and the hope that this generates. We can be caught in a spiritual 'paralysis', unable to move forward because of fixation with the past.

A NEW CREATION

David, the psalmist, had cried out to God: 'Set me free from my prison, that I may praise your name' (Psalm 142:7). He also wrote of God as being the One who 'lifted me out of the slimy pit, out of the mud and mire' (Psalm 40:2). These words reflected his sense of being restricted by afflictions and sin, not being able to move on because of past situations and failures (perhaps recent or longstanding). Paul in the New Testament wrote to Christians who had a particularly 'dark' past. The apostle encouraged them to put this behind them and focus on what God had for them in the future:

> You were taught, with regard to your former way of life, to put off your old self, which is being corrupted by its deceitful desires; to be made new in the attitude of your minds; and to put on the new self, created to be like God in true righteousness and holiness.
>
> (Ephesians 4:22–24)

To another group (also with a dodgy past) Paul was particularly succinct: 'Therefore, if anyone is in Christ, the new creation has come: the old has gone, the new is here!' (2 Corinthians 5:17).

The Old Testament prophets were also alerted to the new life which God brings:

> Forget the former things;
> do not dwell on the past.
> See, I am doing a new thing!
> Now it springs up; do you not perceived it?
> I am making a way in the wilderness
> and streams in the wasteland.
>
> (Isaiah 43:18–19)

This is what the LORD Almighty says: 'In this place, desolate and without people or animals – in all its towns there will again be pastures for shepherds to rest their flocks. In the towns of the hill country, of the western foothills and of the Negev, in the territory of Benjamin, in the villages around Jerusalem and in the towns of Judah, flocks will again pass under the hand of the one who counts them,' says the LORD.

> (Jeremiah 33:12–13)

GOOD NEWS

The above verses had an initial application to the Israelites. They were being freed from captivity in exile and allowed to return to their homeland from which they had been previously driven on account of spiritual failure. But they also provide a 'picture' that relates to us. Jesus' life, death and resurrection means that we are released from the grip of sin and bondage of the past. He spoke of this in His 'manifesto' at the beginning of His ministry (reading from Isaiah 61:1–2):

> The Spirit of the Lord is on me,
> because he has anointed me

to proclaim good news to the poor.
He has sent me to proclaim freedom for the
prisoners
and recovery of sight for the blind,
to set the oppressed free,
to proclaim the year of the Lord's favour.

(Luke 4:18–19)

Jesus underlined the application of those prophetic words to Himself: 'He began by saying to them, "Today this scripture is fulfilled in your hearing"' (Luke 4:21). Jesus brought hope in declaring that our future does not have to be determined by our past failure or, indeed, that of others who have impacted our lives.

Jesus brought hope

DIVINE ENCOUNTER

The former politician, Jonathan Aitken, was brought a sense of this release and reassurance by God when at a crucial stage in his life. Having resigned from his government post as Chief Secretary to the Treasury in order to pursue libel proceedings in the courts, he was prosecuted for perjury. In a riveting description of this unfolding situation, his autographical account Pride and Perjury (Harper Collins, 2000) includes details of what could be understood as a divine encounter. This took place when Aitken was walking along a beach in Kent pending his court hearing. He sensed a voice telling him to slow down, keep on the road ahead, to keep praying and trying to find the way. The events of the past, while not being possible to discard (and prosecuting barristers would ensure no stone was left unturned!), were not to distract him from what lay ahead. Although he was to lose his money, marriage, political career and freedom (he was subsequently found guilty and imprisoned), he didn't allow these events to distract him from growing in his faith.

NO PRECEDENT

Jesus' perspective on time in general, and the past in particular, was therefore very different from that of his disciples. Instead of deliberating on events which had taken place, He knew that His 'work' was to bring spiritual liberation for what lay ahead. The actual healing of this blind man took place to an extent that had no precedent in the Gospel accounts – a pair of functioning eyes were created where none had ever previously existed. Jesus went completely outside of expectations based on the past. 'He spat on the ground, made some mud with the saliva, and put it on the man's eyes' (John 9:6). He then told the man to wash in the Pool of Siloam, which then resulted in him coming home seeing. It has been suggested that the mud placed on the man's eyes contained the very DNA of God so that (as in Genesis 2:7) He was creating something out of dust – in this case a set of fully functioning eyes.

SPIRITUAL IMPACT

Through the healing of this blind man there was also a clear and unequivocal statement to the Jewish religious leaders that Jesus was the Christ. Their teaching wanted to hold this man in spiritual 'chains' to the past. That's why their subsequent investigation and interrogation of the man himself and his parents initially tried to deny that any miracle had taken place at all. When that approach failed – the parents verifying their son's congenital condition – they took the angle that this miracle was of God alone. They definitely did not want to attribute it to Jesus as that would point to Him being divine. Instead they declared Him a 'sinner' (probably on the grounds that the miracle had been performed on the sacred Sabbath). But the man who was healed refused to accept these contentions, holding on to the conviction that Jesus had opened his eyes. This so infuriated those Pharisees that, in asserting that they were the disciples of Moses – which was again seriously placing them back in the past – they ended up throwing the man out of the synagogue and the religious fellowship.

But this was not actually bad news as far as the man was concerned. That's because he experienced not only a physical change, but also a deep spiritual impact. The conclusion of John's account describes him meeting with Jesus, who revealed Himself as the Son of God. The healed man responded: 'Lord, I believe.' He then 'worshipped him' (John 9:38). This intervention of Jesus was not the only one that resulted in the grip and stigma of people's pasts being removed, meaning that they were free to move on. Mary Magdalene, Zacchaeus, the woman at the well of Samaria, Peter, the woman caught in adultery, Matthew and many others also had particular pasts, full of regret, but from which Jesus released them.

GRIP OF THE PAST
We all need to be broken free from elements of the past in order to look forward in time and receive the new life that Christ gives us through His death on the cross. A story is told of a man, centuries ago, being branded. He had been convicted of being a sheep thief and so the letters 'S' and 'T' were burned on his forehead. But he subsequently had an experience of God which

completely changed his behaviour and attitude. This was so dramatic that, thereafter, people saw those letters and thought that they were an abbreviation of the word 'Saint'. God has the power to remove the grip of the past and bring hope for the future.

* * *

REFLECTION

Grounds for hope (as seen in this chapter):

- Jesus was not prepared to assess a person's condition but then leave them in an afflicted state.
- Jesus declared that our future did not have to be determined by past failure, either our own failure or that of others who have impacted our lives.
- Jesus was able to go completely outside of expectations and precedent.

POINTS TO PONDER

1. What possible reasons exist for our lives to be gripped by the past? Tick as many boxes as apply.

   We fail to realise the impact that the past may have exerted on us ☐

   We don't feel that anything can be done to free us from the past ☐

   We fear the consequences of moving into 'unknown territory' ☐

   We don't want to make the effort needed to face up to the past before moving on ☐

   We feel that the past is too valuable to discard ☐

2. What attitudes and thought patterns are likely to be affected by events and influences from the past, particularly when we were children and growing up?

3. What is the importance of knowing that Jesus can interact in our lives in totally unexpected and unprecedented ways? How can we be more open to experiencing this?

4. In what ways can we be encouraged in knowing that we are, as Christians, a 'new creation ... the old has gone, the new is here' (2 Corinthians 5:17)?

5. What situations or influences that grip you from the past are you needing to bring to Jesus, so that you can experience Him working in your life to bring freedom and healing?

9

GOD – ON HOLD?

'Lord,' Martha said to Jesus, 'if you had been here, my brother would not have died.'

(John 11:21)

Read: John 11:1–44

'Sorry you've been kept waiting' is the usual comment made by the lady in my bank when I'm eventually summoned to her counter. In fact the queue that I initially joined, or the time that it took for my turn, may not have been particularly long. But her statement is clearly part of 'customer service' training that instructs the bank's employees to apologise first before ascertaining what help is required – presumably enhancing the 'customer experience'. It's a situation that most of us can usually handle because we can physically observe what's going on.

An entirely different scenario arises when phone contact is attempted with a bank or big organisation. To negotiate a succession of options only to be informed, by a dismembered automated voice, that 'You are in a queue', followed by, 'Please hold for an advisor', is not easy. But harder still is the periodic incantation: 'Sorry to keep you waiting. Your call is important to us.' Am I the only one who struggles to keep calm in response to such banality, resisting the urge to shout back something I might not want aired in public? If my call is so important then why doesn't the bank (or whoever) employ and train more staff to answer phone calls within a reasonable time – like straight away?

A SHOCK!

Banks – so we are told – together with government bodies and big organisations, aim to minimise waiting times and apologise for delays. God does not. That may come as a surprise or a shock. It's not what we've come to expect in our 'customer-focused' and 'joined-up' world. It's almost become a right for us not to have to wait for anything. If we are forced to do so, we are given the expectation of an apology, immediate attention... and compensation. But with God it's different. Waiting and spending time without seeing anything happen – without even an expression of regret or explanation – is sometimes the way God works. So we have to learn to change that normal response of hurt pride, frustration and anger. Such reactions are not going to help. Nor will they make God 'hurry up' or change His timescale, whatever our situation or schedule. God, as it may be termed, sometimes puts us 'on hold'.

MANAGING EXPECTATIONS

That's the scenario Martha and Mary faced. They were certainly under pressure. Theirs was literally a life-or-death issue. It related

GOD – ON HOLD?

to their brother, Lazarus, who was very sick. So timing wasn't about convenience or simply accomplishing a task and moving on. A man's life was at stake. In view of this the sisters probably expected an immediate response from Jesus to whom they had forwarded this information. Their message was succinct: 'Lord, the one you love is ill' (John 11:3).

The sisters anticipated that any teaching or preaching appointments, any healing mission or other miracle opportunities, would be immediately curtailed by Jesus. Almost certainly their expectation was that He would 'hotfoot' it to their village, Bethany, just outside Jerusalem. But Jesus, upon receiving this message, did not move an inch. This wasn't because of the need to fulfil His schedule, or because he didn't care about Lazarus, Martha and Mary. Indeed it is specifically recorded: 'Now Jesus loved Martha and her sister and Lazarus' (John 11:5).

Any doubt as to Jesus' intention regarding this pressured situation was dispelled by the next statement: 'So when he heard that Lazarus was ill, he stayed where he was two more days' (John 11:6). Jesus was not confused about what was happening. Nor was he preoccupied with a demanding schedule. Being in full possession of the facts (including that Lazarus was about to die by this time), Jesus stayed where He was. Those 'expectations' held by the sisters would have to be 'managed'.

They were definitely put on hold.

CAN YOU SERIOUSLY BELIEVE IT?

As events would prove, the sisters failed to manage their expectations. But we are most likely to join them in that respect!

That's because the action, or seeming inaction, of Jesus in this account is so counter-intuitive to our modern-day approach that we can probably scarcely believe what we're reading. Words such as 'now', 'don't hang around', 'deadlines', 'quick response' and 'flagged up for action' totally colour our attitude. This type of thinking – that we are owed prompt action – has been around a long time. It was actually enshrined in the Magna Carta of 1215, meaning that it even preceded the Bill of Rights or the European Court of Human Rights! Specifically it stated: 'To no man will we sell, or deny *or delay right* or justice' (emphasis mine). So there we have it. No wonder we get upset when action doesn't happen promptly.

Moreover, lack of action, especially on the part of God, causes us to ask whether He is fully aware of pressing situations. It makes us question if God truly realises that there are occasions when we need His intervention immediately – if not sooner. We can start to doubt if He really loves and cares for us. Any number of circumstances can generate these, and similar, questions in our minds. The situation facing Martha and Mary was the most extreme: Lazarus' condition was life-threatening.

Jesus gave only one explanation for His decision to remain where He was and not travel to Judea straight away. We had better listen carefully, because this is something we also need to hear. He said: 'This illness will not end in death. No, it is for God's glory so that God's Son may be glorified through it' (John 11:4). Now this response is also something we probably find difficult to stomach. That's because even as Christians we are heavily (and covertly) influenced by the 'selfie' and 'how-

We had better listen carefully

88

many-Facebook-Friends-like-my-postings?' mentality that surrounds us. As a result we subconsciously, or otherwise, feel that God's intervention – preferably miraculous and speedy – is owed to us; that it's a 'given'. We tend to see things in terms of God working for our blessing and benefit; He has promised to do it – end of argument!

GOD'S GLORY – NOT OUR SELF-CENTREDNESS

Now it is true that God's love means that, as our Heavenly Father, He cares for us, provides for our needs, and answers prayer in more ways than we appreciate. But, ultimately, there is a reason over and above these others as to why He may respond by seemingly doing nothing when we are in need of help. John's narrative brings out the fact that Jesus' work of miraculous intervention is done so that He is 'glorified'. This means that His love, power, wisdom and sovereign control in all circumstances are revealed and no longer obscured. The word 'glorified' in the original text pointed to the splendour, radiance and majesty of God... not our self-centred satisfaction.

Actually we shouldn't be surprised about this aim that lay behind Jesus' work. The apostle Paul was another New Testament writer who seemed to be captivated by what 'being glorified' meant, referring to it four times in his opening chapter of the letter to the Ephesians: 'to the praise of His glorious grace ... in order that we, who were the first to put our hope in Christ, might be for the praise of his glory ... to the praise of his glory ... the glorious Father' (Ephesians 1:6, 12, 14, 17).

John's Gospel repeatedly uses that word 'glory' in respect of Jesus, an ongoing reminder to us. John's first chapter encapsulates this fact:

In the beginning was the Word, and the Word was with God, and the Word was God ... The Word became flesh and made his dwelling among us. We have seen his glory, the glory of the one and only Son, who came from the Father, full of grace and truth.

(John 1:1, 14)

A DIFFERENT AGENDA

As previously mentioned in respect of His first miracle, only a few people were aware of Jesus turning water into wine. But the disciples of Jesus were among them, and John linked this to Jesus being 'glorified': 'What Jesus did here in Cana of Galilee was the first of the signs through which he revealed his glory; and his disciples believed in him' (John 2:11). Many other references point to Jesus and His 'glory' in relation to His Father (see John 5:41; 5:44; 7:18; 8:50; 8:54; 12:41; 17:5: 17:22; 17:24). By delaying His journey and eventual arrival in Bethany, Jesus was going to reveal His glory in acting on a different agenda from what was anticipated. He was not going to bring health to a sick man, but resurrection life to a dead one.

This scenario regarding delay has significant relevance to us, and not only in terms of physical health. There may be occasions when our hopes, dreams, aspirations and ambitions, sincerely held and prayed about, eventually wither and 'die'... and end up 'buried'. Many causes may contribute to such an ending, but time will always be a factor. As time progresses, so the options and opportunities may decrease, energy and ability may lessen, support may drop away, and resources may diminish. This loss can impact us deeply, as the writer of Proverbs stated: 'Hope deferred makes the heart sick' (Proverbs 13:12).

GOD'S TIMELINE

Jesus not only declared that 'God's Son [would] be glorified' through this situation. He added a further element to being 'glorified' when, after the two days had passed, He set out for Judea. The disciples had questioned this decision because there had been a recent attempt by the Jews in that area to seize and stone Him (John 10:31, 39). In response to that question, Jesus talked about time:

> Are there not twelve hours of daylight? Anyone who walks in the day-time will not stumble, for they see by this world's light. It is when a person walks at night that they stumble, for they have no light.
>
> (John 11:9–10)

Jesus was bringing an illustration to confirm that there was a particular and definite 'timeline' in His work by which He was being glorified. This timeline would not be shortened or altered by the actions or intentions of His enemies... or anyone else.

Again this is applicable to us as we endeavour to walk closely with God. He has a timeline that determines our lives and their length. The psalmist knew that the days of his life were 'ordained' by God (Psalm 139:16). He also declared:

> LORD, you alone are my portion and my cup;
> you make my lot secure.
> The boundary lines have fallen for me in pleasant places;
> surely I have a delightful inheritance.
>
> (Psalm 16:5–6)

Moses prophesied about one of the tribes that God would work so that 'your strength will equal your days' (Deuteronomy 33:25). In the words of the hymn writer:

> Not a single shaft can hit,
> till the God of love sees fit.
> (from the hymn 'Sovereign Ruler of the
> Skies' by John Ryland, 1753–1825)

ANOTHER SHOCK

But then Jesus, preparing to set out on this journey, made things clear to His disciples – that they were going to the place where Lazarus lived (not just the general area of Judea) and that Lazarus was dead. It was that last fact that probably brought a shocked reaction. That's because, moments previously, Jesus had stated that Lazarus had 'fallen asleep' but that He was going to 'wake him up' (John 11:11). But such terminology simply showed how He had viewed the situation. His divine power and authority meant that raising someone from the dead was, to Him, just like waking up a sleeping person!

ARRIVAL – AT LAST

Jesus and His disciples arrived in Bethany to find confirmation of what He had been previously told. Lazarus was dead, already having been in the tomb for four days. (Burial would have taken place very soon after death.) Again the 'time' element was a factor in what took place. In purely practical terms it meant that decomposition of the body would have commenced. Martha was subsequently to comment about conditions in that tomb: 'By this time there is a bad odour' (John 11:39). But there was also a rabbinical tradition that the soul of a deceased person hovered around the body for three days before departing, once decomposition was underway. Although Bible commentators aren't certain as to when this tradition originated, the length of time since Lazarus' death was not in dispute. Lazarus was seriously dead! His was not a very recent death as had been the case with the two other resurrections that Jesus brought about – Jairus' daughter and the widow of Nain's son (Luke 8:49–56; 7:11–15).

HE HAS THE LAST WORD!

Although Jesus had now arrived in Bethany, there was yet a further delay in His intervention regarding Lazarus. The raising from the dead was preceded by Jesus' words of confirming, crying, commanding and calling out. This further element of delay may, again, surprise us. Our expectation is geared to seeing God 'do something' without delay as we sense His presence. But this account again reveals a different agenda and timeline. It particularly involved dialogue... and showed that Jesus had the last word.

Firstly, Jesus was met by Martha. She clearly believed that Jesus was the Christ, the Son of God. This was affirmed following Jesus' words of confirmation: 'I am the resurrection and the life. The one who believes in me will live, even though they die; and whoever lives by believing in me will never die' (John 11:25–26). The initial part of what Jesus stated concerning the believer was in the context of those who had died, while the second part was in relation to those believers still alive. Both statements rested on the truth of Jesus being the wellspring of life. It seemed that Martha needed to grasp the truth that belief in Jesus and His power over death was not an abstract or distant hope, but was a present reality.

Mary then spoke to Jesus, after coming out of her home to which Martha had returned. Her opening words were the same as her sister's: 'Lord, if you had been here, my brother would not have died' (John 11:32; see 11:21). Those were the only words she spoke. Having fallen at Jesus' feet she was also weeping. Were they tears erupting from her dashed hopes of Jesus bringing healing? Whatever the reason, it is recorded that Jesus Himself, seeing the Jews with her also weeping, 'was deeply moved in spirit and troubled' (John 11:33). Upon being shown where Lazarus had been laid, His response was to cry: 'Jesus wept' (John 11:35). His loving and caring sympathy, identifying with those sisters, could only be adequately expressed in tears.

DEFINITE STEP FORWARD

Jesus' intimate conversations with Martha and Mary confirming His power and love were a necessary prelude to what happened next. The delay in talking with the sisters had meant that their relationship with Him was deepened. Perhaps only those tragic circumstances could have caused this to happen. Jesus' delays are not without purpose.

So finally the words of command and calling out by Jesus brought about His glorification. Jesus had the 'last word' in this situation… as He does in all others! Commanding that the stone be rolled away from the tomb, He first called upon His Father before calling out: 'Lazarus, come out!' (John 11:43). Lazarus was resurrected from the dead… Many of the Jews, when they saw what Jesus had done, 'believed in him' (11:45), and from that day the religious leaders plotted to take Jesus' life. What had initially been a delay ended as a definite step forward in God's purposes being carried out. Jesus' timeline may not have been obvious to those affected by it, but through experiencing that delay, more was achieved in the lives of many individuals than might otherwise have been the case, and Jesus Himself was glorified through it.

* * *

REFLECTION

Grounds for hope (as seen in this chapter):

- Jesus was fully aware of the pressing situation regarding Lazarus and his impending death.
- Jesus works in everything so that He is glorified.
- Jesus has a timeline that determines our lives and their length.
- Jesus has the final word in every situation – even death.

POINTS TO PONDER

1. Why are we likely to get agitated when God doesn't seem to respond to us immediately and we consequently experience delays? What do your answers indicate about the way you might view God? Tick as many boxes as apply.

   We feel that God has forgotten us ☐
   We fear that God doesn't care ☐
   We reckon that God is preoccupied with other tasks ☐
   We think that unless God does something now, it will be too late ☐
   We consider that we haven't prayed enough and God hasn't heard us ☐

2. Why do we struggle to understand that all Jesus does is ultimately so that He is glorified? How can we become less self-centred, and more Jesus-centred, in our attitude?

3. What other examples in the Bible involved a (seeming) delay in God intervening in answer to the prayers of His people?

4. How can we deepen our trust in God even when we experience delays with regard to His intervention?

5. In what situation are you experiencing delay regarding God answering prayer, and what do you feel He is showing you as you wait for His clear intervention?

POSTSCRIPT 1
JUST ANOTHER DAY?

One day Peter and John were going up to the temple at the time of
prayer – at three in the afternoon.

(Acts 3:1)

Read: Acts 3:1–10

'How is your week going?' That's a question that's likely to receive a detailed reply only if something particularly exciting, unusual or startling has occurred. Let's face it, no one's going to be interested in the normal and routine. These probably occupy most of our time. Even a work scenario is unlikely to attract much attention unless the questioner has an interest in our line of work... or the Official Secrets Act forbids disclosure! Facebook postings epitomise this attitude – it's the intriguing, unusual and picturesque events that attract those 'likes'.

In view of that situation, we don't necessarily place much value on things that are commonplace – the job, shopping, household chores, checking emails, or even going to church, among a huge volume of other tasks we undertake. Nothing exciting about those things, is there? They may take up time, energy and resources, but they don't constitute any real interest to outsiders. In terms of replying to that initial question, probably most of us would give a brief reply before moving on to more interesting matters.

NOTHING UNUSUAL

So when the Acts of the Apostles (chapter 3) begins, 'One day Peter and John were going up to the temple ...' there is nothing to alert us to anything special that's about to take place. It may, of course, also be the case that this part of the Bible is familiar to us anyway and so we know what's about to erupt. We are therefore not surprised by what takes place, even though when we first read the account we may have been thrilled! But, trying to put ourselves in the place of onlookers at that time, there's actually nothing to suggest the amazing events that are to follow. It's a common scene: two men striding (or ambling, looking around, perhaps) towards the place of worship in Jerusalem.

REVOLUTION... AND ROUTINE

Before we go any further it's necessary to pick up on what's happened so far. Jesus was no longer physically present with His disciples. Following His death and resurrection He had ascended to heaven. However, before the ascension took place He had instructed His followers to remain in Jerusalem. They were to wait for the 'gift my Father promised' (Acts 1:4). Time was an essential element in what God was doing. On the day of Pentecost, having waited, these followers were baptised with the Holy Spirit. This, as Peter (the apostle) subsequently pointed out, was the fulfilment of Old Testament prophecy from probably around six centuries previously. The time had now come:

'In the last days,' God says,
'I will pour out my Spirit on all people.
Your sons and daughters will prophesy,
your young men will see visions,
your old men will dream dreams.
Even on my servants, both men and women,
I will pour out my Spirit in those days,
and they will prophesy.'

(Acts 2:17–18; quoting from Joel 2:28–29)

Previously, as we have seen, time had been an essential element of Jesus' ministry even though it was not necessarily obvious. Although He was now ascended, the work of God's Holy Spirit through His followers was to continue to feature 'time' in what was taking place… and it still does!

The sermon that Peter subsequently preached on the day of Pentecost had massive reverberations. The Holy Spirit was at work, with the result that 'about three thousand' people were added to the number of original believers (Acts 2:41). Their lifestyle and the accompanying 'signs and wonders' arising from being filled with the Holy Spirit culminated in further growth being seen: 'And the Lord added to their number daily those who were being saved' (Acts 2:47).

But this new way of life by those in the early Church involved not only revolution (in both spiritual and material terms) but also routine. 'Every day they continued to meet together in the temple courts. They broke bread in their homes and ate together with glad and sincere hearts' (Acts 2:46). Although the temple may have been associated with the Jewish religious leaders who had plotted to kill Jesus and would then attempt (as time was to show) to eradicate the propagation of His teaching, there was nothing to prevent devout Jews from entering that building complex. On that basis the followers of Christ continued the routine of going up there to meet and pray.

The closing section of Acts chapter 2 does not specify the further numbers by which the Church was increased following Pentecost. But it is important to note how these early Christians (as they were eventually labelled) adopted a certain pattern. There can be a tendency to follow the world's formula in church life by concentrating on organising eye-catching events and high-profile activities – all put on social media in the hope that postings might go viral, naturally. God may direct us to use such an approach at times. But essentially He has His ways of working through us as His Church. Unbeknown to Peter and John, there was about to be a seismic increase in the number of believers and the overall impact of the Church... all because they were carrying on with their normal routine.

A SCHEDULE...

Going up to the temple was a regular practice for every devout Jew. It was customary for Jews to pray three times a day, as exemplified by Daniel, the Old Testament prophet:

Now when Daniel learned that the decree had been published, he went home to his upstairs room where the windows opened towards Jerusalem. Three times a day he

got down on his knees and prayed, giving thanks to his God,
just as he had done before.

(Daniel 6:10)

Similarly the psalmist recorded: 'Evening, morning and noon I
cry out in distress, and he hears my voice' (Psalm 55:17). These
timings were reflected in particular events described in the Acts
of the Apostles. The time that the disciples were filled with the
Holy Spirit at Pentecost was nine o' clock in the morning (Acts
2:15). Peter went up onto the roof of his house to pray at noon
(Acts 10:9). And here we read of Peter and John going to the
temple at 'three in the afternoon'.

On the backdrop of this schedule of prayer, having been
carried out for many years, something entirely unforeseen was to
emerge. There was nothing to suggest that anything was going
to be different. No record was made of these apostles having
previously received any specific prophetic word, dream, vision or
other supernatural prompting about that day. All of which means
that we should not shun or despise the routines of life, especially
those arising from our relationship with God. It was when
William Booth was undertaking a routine-type activity of walking
– in his case, through London in 1865 – that his spiritual 'eyes'
were opened to what was around him in the East End. The
impact was so deep that he returned home to his wife and
declared: 'Darling, I've found my destiny.' It was that ordinary
task that led to the formation of the Salvation Army.

...A COMMON SCENE...

But there was another routine that was being carried out that day.
Again it was not something that would have attracted the least bit
of notice. A man, disabled from birth, was carried out to the

temple gate, 'where he was put every day to beg from those going into the temple courts' (Acts 3:3). His presence in that location was a daily feature... as was the need for him to be carried. He was in a totally helpless condition. This crippled man's location, probably at the entrance to the inner temple, has led to the suggestion that the disciples – even Jesus – would probably have seen him on many previous occasions. The scene that is set out was therefore an entirely common one – a beggar in a desperate situation, and two men going to pray. It was just another day.

Most of us, much of the time, go through what we might describe as 'just another day'. Keith White, the author and director of a residential Christian community caring for children and families in East London, writes of such periods. When returning from the USSR in 1989 after witnessing the imminent break-up of the Soviet Union, he reflected:

> Despite our interest in and commitment to Christians in Russia, we both felt our vocation was to live and serve in the comparatively uneventful life of England. And as I pondered this contrast I realised that it is the calling of most Christians most of the time, whether we live in periods of great upheaval or stability, to be faithful and responsible in the ordinary, mundane affairs of daily existence.

Keith also pointed out:

> Of course we treasure the special times and we celebrate the extraordinary events, but it is not healthy to assure that they are, or to long that they should be, the staple spiritual and emotional diet of our lives.

> (quoted from Keith J. White, *In the Meantime* [WTL Publications, 2013], pp. 9, 11 – used with permission)

However, into this ordinary and commonplace scene, with no indication of anything about to take place... God moved.

...AN ORDINARY REQUEST...

Even on the brink of God's extraordinary intervention there was nothing unusual taking place. The disabled man simply did what he always did when seeing people go up to the temple: 'When he saw Peter and John about to enter, he asked them for money' (Acts 3:3). He requested money... but he received a miracle.

...AND AN EXTRAORDINARY SEQUEL

However, Peter's response was not what was expected. His words could only be attributed to the fact that he was 'filled with the Holy Spirit'. In the next chapter of Acts it is recorded: 'Then Peter, filled with the Holy Spirit ... And they were all [including Peter] filled with the Holy Spirit ... With great power the apostles [including Peter] continued to testify to the resurrection of the Lord Jesus' (Acts 4:8, 31, 33). It was the Spirit of God who filled Peter and alerted him to the fact that there was something more that could be done for this disabled man. This was no longer an 'ordinary' scenario.

But before Peter actually spoke to the man, the narrative states that 'Peter looked straight at him, as did John' (Acts 4:4). The word 'looked' in the original language was one used almost exclusively by Luke in his accounts. It brings a sense of intensity and focus. Peter used that word himself: 'Why do you stare at us ...?' (Acts 3:12). It was also used in respect of the martyr Stephen: 'But Stephen, full of the Holy Spirit, looked up' (Acts 7:55) and of Paul, 'Then ... Paul, filled with the Holy Spirit, looked straight at Elymas' (Acts 13:9). This act of looking was more than a physical activity;

it was linked with spiritual discernment. Everyone else simply saw a crippled man... but Peter saw a man and saw that it was the time for an extraordinary intervention of God. This is a lesson for us. Instead of spending hours staring at our smartphone or computer, let's spend more time being sensitive to God, reflecting on the Bible, and hearing His 'take' on what's around us.

Peter instructed the man, in turn, to give them his full attention. He then declared: 'Silver or gold I do not have, but what I do have I give you. In the name of Jesus Christ of Nazareth, walk' (Acts 3:6). These words were not spoken out of the blue. Peter had been impacted, through the Holy Spirit, by the promises of Jesus. These included:

> Go into all the world and preach the gospel to all creation ... And these signs will accompany those who believe: in my name they will drive out demons; they will speak in new tongues; they will pick up snakes with their hands; and when they drink deadly poison, it will not hurt them at all; they will place their hands on people who are ill, and they will get well.
>
> (Mark 16:15, 17–18)

Mark's account had described the disciples as previously experiencing the power of God in bringing healing: 'They went out and preached that people should repent. They drove out many demons and anointed with oil many people who were ill and healed them' (Mark 6:12–13).

SPIRITUAL CHANGE...

Having spoken those words, Peter then helped the disabled man to his feet. 'Instantly the man's feet and ankles became strong'

(Acts 3:7). He consequently 'jumped' to his feet and began to walk. Luke, being a medical expert, was careful to pinpoint the anatomical area where his disability existed... and was now amazingly changed! The man, perhaps instinctively, knew what to do next. He joined Peter and John, and entered the temple courts. But this was not a quiet and unobtrusive event! He was 'walking and jumping, and praising God' (Acts 3:9).

The outcome of this healing and dramatic demonstration of God's power through the name of Jesus was not long in emerging. What had begun as a routine and regular feature at that time of the day – people passing a crippled man on their way into the temple – ended very differently! There was another great spiritual change. The crippled beggar, now clearly seen jumping and praising God, was recognised by 'all the people' (Acts 3:11). Their reaction – being 'astonished' – enabled Peter to preach another sermon pointing to Jesus as the Christ. The result was a further growth in the number of those who became believers: 'many who heard the message believed; so the number of men who believed grew to about five thousand' (Acts 4:4). The translation of that phrase, 'to about', is apparently not clear. It could mean either that the number of total believers grew to that number, or that the figure was the number added as a result of that day's miracle and preaching.

...AND A THROWAWAY REMARK

However, what is made very clear was the reaction of certain other people, namely the religious leaders, who had Peter and John seized and put in jail until the next day. During the subsequent hearing before the high priest and other members of the hierarchy, Peter delivered a forthright declaration regarding 'Jesus Christ of Nazareth' (see Acts 4:8–12). Three aspects were particularly noted about the eventful 24 hours that had passed. Firstly, it was clear that Peter and John were men of courage – they did not hold anything back – something that even the religious leaders recognised . Secondly, those leaders acknowledged that these two men were 'unschooled, ordinary men'. And this meant that, thirdly, their actions and power could only be explained by the fact that they 'had been with Jesus' (Acts 4:13). Peter and John were therefore released, after being warned not to speak or teach 'in the name of Jesus' (4:18).

But, finally, the aspect that seemed to have caused the religious leaders real problems – not knowing how to properly deal with Peter and John – was an issue relating to time. Almost as a 'throwaway' remark, Luke states at the end of this account: 'For the man who was miraculously healed was over forty years old' (Acts 4:22). Perhaps Luke was wearing his 'doctor's hat' again, implying that a man of that age, disabled for that length of time, could not normally expect any medical change in his condition. It was that combination that 'threw' those leaders. But it was not a situation that 'threw' God, or prevented Him from intervening. He did so, not only in a situation that seemed, on the surface, totally commonplace and routine, but also at a point in time when the age threshold of the person concerned seemed to have long passed.

William Carey, the pioneer missionary to India who travelled to the subcontinent from England in 1793 and never returned home, was used by God in amazing ways to share the good news of Jesus. It is reported that he attributed his work to one characteristic: 'I can plod.' The times of routine activity and plodding may not indicate any major advance, but God can bring extraordinary change in times of ordinary events.

* * *

REFLECTION

Grounds for hope (as seen in this chapter):

- The routines of daily life are not to be considered as having no value.
- God honours our commitment to Him, even in ordinary circumstances.
- God can bring extraordinary change in times of ordinary events.

POINTS TO PONDER

1. Why are we likely to feel that nothing extraordinary will happen in the daily mundane and ordinary tasks we undertake? What do your answers indicate about your view of the ordinary and mundane aspects of life? Tick as many boxes as apply.

   We feel that God isn't interested in our ordinary circumstances ☐

   We reckon there's no potential for anything extraordinary to occur ☐

   We operate in 'automatic mode' and don't notice any possible alternatives ☐

   We don't feel that we 'qualify' for any extraordinary intervention from God ☐

   We consider that our circumstances are far too mundane ☐

2. What are some of the 'positives' in having a routine and settled way of doing things in our daily lives?

3. What steps can we take to be more open and alert to the opportunities that God may want to open up to us in our routine activity?

4. How can we develop the ability to listen to what other people say to us, and use their questions and comments as a 'springboard' for God to be brought into the conversation?

5. Into what mundane and routine activity can you specifically pray that God would intervene in such a way that His extraordinary power is somehow clearly demonstrated?

POSTSCRIPT 2
IN BETWEEN

In Damascus there was a disciple named Ananias. The Lord called to
him in a vision, 'Ananias!' 'Yes, Lord,' he answered.

(Acts 9:10)

Read: Acts 9:9–19

'A Damascus Road experience'. This is a frequently used phrase that appears even in today's secular and postmodernist environment. But its origin is entirely biblical, recorded in Acts 9:1–8. It relates to the conversion experience of a man named Saul who was subsequently to be used by God as a major apologist for Christianity. The event that gave rise to this expression was a totally unexpected and blinding light from heaven which came to him while he was en route to Damascus; during this experience Saul was confronted with the risen Lord Jesus, resulting in a complete change of his mind and spirit. Previously

Saul had been intent on destroying Christianity and all those who followed Jesus. Afterwards he emerged as a preacher and apostle, founding many churches and wholly committed to Jesus Christ. So it's not surprising that when someone's viewpoint or attitude is transformed, perhaps by a particular event, the person is described as having undergone such a 'Damascus Road experience'.

This experience may last only moments. What is often not realised is that in Saul's case there was an essential 'follow-up' element. His encounter with Jesus had totally changed his outlook, and he now acknowledged that Jesus was the Christ, the 'Righteous One' (Acts 22:14). However, the experience on that road had left him physically blinded, and not wanting (perhaps unable) to eat or drink. More importantly, there was a huge spiritual impact that needed to be worked through.

THE 'TIME' ELEMENT

Linked to these aspects of Saul's experience was the element of time. The account in Acts simply describes Saul being led in a helpless condition into Damascus and lying in a room in the house of a man named Judas situated on Straight Street. He was in that state, seemingly uninterrupted, for three days. This was an 'in between' time. It was not a period about which God was either ignorant or oblivious. Neither were they days simply to be ticked off the calendar before getting to a point where things really started to happen. Saul, having been renamed 'Paul' and subsequently writing many of the books of the New Testament – letters to different groups of Christians – never directly referred to this period. The only disclosure about those three days was that he was 'praying' (Acts 9:11). With no visual distraction on account of blindness, abstinence from food, seemingly left alone with all appointments (presumably) cancelled, being in prayer with God was a necessary activity.

SHAPING THE FUTURE

That initial period, once over, saw Saul spending several days with the disciples in Damascus. In addition, 'At once he began to preach in the synagogues that Jesus is the Son of God' (Acts 9:20). This preaching was ongoing. Clearly those three days were important, being a time that shaped Saul's future. Firstly, it showed that God was not in a rush for Paul (as Saul was subsequently called; Acts 13:9) to be engaged in his apostolic travelling, preaching and writing. These ministries were to be worked out at God's pace and timing. Those roles would take place in ways that were not necessarily straightforward in the years ahead. But for the moment, immediately following his conversion, Saul was living through this 'in between' time and working through the spiritual effects of that encounter with Jesus. The words that Saul had heard on the Damascus Road – 'Saul, Saul, why do you persecute me?' (Acts 9:4) – radically changed his understanding, and needed a serious response which involved time.

EXAMPLES FROM NATURE AND MEDICINE

In our own age, and even in the church environment, there always seems to be a drive for people to 'move on', 'move up a gear', face the next 'challenge', 'tick off' another 'box', and rise to the 'next level'. No time is seemingly left in which to pause, take stock, and await God's timing and resourcing. Nature, when we stop to notice, cannot be rushed. The changing of the seasons, the need to allow ground to lie fallow, the dark and cold winter months preventing much human involvement (or interference) in the growing process... all of these point to time being given for nature to take its course.

Even in the field of medical science it's acknowledged that allowance has to be made for the human body to recover and restore loss of function at a pace largely decided by nature. Whatever medical intervention may be possible or appropriate, there is always a 'process' which needs to be navigated. Sometimes we learn the hard way that time has to be given for healing to take place. Jogging has long been one of my main forms of exercise. Although I've never achieved marathon distances, my shorter runs (dependent upon the weather, my energy levels and motivation!) feature fairly regularly in my week. But on one occasion, nearing the end of a run, I unaccountably pulled up with a strain. 'Running it off' didn't help, nor did a few days' rest. The internet pinpointed the cause of the problem – and indicated that several weeks' rest was probably necessary. The latter advice, of course, I ignored. But that was to my cost... and discomfort. The legs – by this time the other one had decided it was also going to sustain a strain – were telling me to 'lay off'. So I had to respond to nature's timetable, take quite a lot of time out, and only resume with shorter and (even) slower runs until I could build up to a normal distance. The speed, however, is still lacking!

Our lives as Christians also need to have 'in between' times for spiritual rest and reflection. The provision of increasing numbers of Christian retreat facilities in the UK is evidence of this being recognised. This is not just applicable for those in full-time Christian work, since all of us need periods in which we can reassess our relationship with God.

an issue of trust since we cannot always see either that bigger picture or the identity of those whom God is 'steering' into position. This was particularly the case with a woman named Gladys Aylward who, in the early 1920s, believed that God was calling her to work for Him as a missionary in China. But her approach to the China Inland Mission, at that time the major organiser of mission from the UK to that country, resulted in failure. Her training was cut short when it was assessed that she did not have the linguistic or academic ability deemed necessary. She was advised to return to her work as a parlour maid, ironically caring for a retired missionary couple. But then God worked so that she heard of an older lady, Jennie Lawson, a widow who had returned to China as a missionary, intending to end her days there. She invited Gladys to travel out to join her and form part of her team, regardless of the young woman's rejection by officialdom and complete lack of 'sponsorship' by any church or organisation. This was the beginning of many events in which God worked through Gladys after she succeeded in travelling overland to the Yancheng district in the west of China. Indeed such was the impact of her eventual work – primarily in leading a hundred orphaned children on a journey of around 200 miles to safety during the Sino-Japanese war in 1938 – that Hollywood made a film about it, The Inn of the Sixth Happiness (1958). Again, this would not have happened had not God brought about an unexpected connection.

Who is it that God wants to bring you into contact with at the right time by which something more of His purposes in your life are worked out?

* * *

117

REFLECTION

Grounds for hope (as seen in this chapter):

- 'In between' times are not periods about which God is ignorant or oblivious.
- They are times which God uses to shape our future.
- God works 'behind the scenes' to bring significant people to impact our lives.

POINTS TO PONDER

1. Why are we likely to feel that 'in between' times don't have much value or purpose?

   There is nothing dramatic or amazing taking place ☐
   It's an anti-climax after something obviously important ☐
   No one significant is around to make an impact ☐
   We feel that God hasn't any more work to do in us ☐
   We have a sense of being unable to move on by ourselves ☐

2. Who else in the Bible underwent periods of 'in between' times when nothing much seemed to be happening but God was working behind the scenes?

3. What is the value of having periods when we can step back from activity and engagement, in order to have an 'in between' time?

4. How can the realisation that we are God's handiwork be helpful in realising that it is He who oversees and imposes these 'in between' times?

5. Why is it important to understand that God is working during those 'in between' times to place alongside us other people (whom we may not have previously met)?

6. In what way do you feel you would be helped by experiencing an 'in between' time imposed by God?

POSTSCRIPT 3
BEYOND TODAY

During the night Paul had a vision of a man of Macedonia standing
and begging him, 'Come over to Macedonia and help us.'

(Acts 16:9)

Read: Acts 16:6–12

He didn't seem to have a clue! This might seem a harsh statement in view of the fact that it refers to Paul, the greatest apostle and Christian apologist this world has known. He was inspired to write the foundational documents of the New Testament – letters upon which church doctrine and practice have rested for two thousand years. Yet here we read an account of Paul and his travelling companions reaching a point in their journeying where they were totally bereft of ideas as to what direction to take.

At this point in what is described as Paul's 'second missionary journey' he, with Silas his newly appointed companion, had completed revisiting the groups of Christians in Asia Minor (modern-day Turkey). These were the churches that he had previously founded in circumstances of some hardship. This latest visit had primarily been undertaken in order to deliver a directive from the 'mother' church at Jerusalem regarding standards of behaviour for these new (and mainly non-Jewish) converts. It is recorded that there was a positive response to this series of visits: 'So the churches were strengthened in the faith and grew daily in numbers' (Acts 16:5).

WHERE NEXT?

Having accomplished that task, and also meeting Timothy, a young man who joined Paul and Silas and became Paul's protégé, it was not at all clear as to what direction they were then to take. Although our circumstances are not going to be anything like the situation described in Acts 16, there may be times when, having done the obvious tasks and responsibilities that lie before us, we are unsure of future direction. In that context time becomes an important factor. This refers not so much to a particular time but simply the days and months (or more) that may be ahead of us. We are only too aware that we are confined in time, being not only unable to go back and rectify past mistakes, but also unable to leap forward to view future possibilities.

But Paul's experience brings a clear example of God, who knows both the past and the future, intervening in this kind of situation. God had a plan for Paul by which His purposes were to be carried out. The apostle was of course aware of the general direction that God wanted him to take. As we have seen, God had spoken to him immediately after his conversion through a man named Ananias who said:

The God of our ancestors has chosen you to know his will
and to see the Righteous One and to hear words from his
mouth. You will be his witness to all people of what you
have seen and heard.

(Acts 22:14–15)

We, similarly, know from the Bible about the general direction
and style of living that God wants for us.

FINDING OURSELVES AT 'TROAS'

It was in that mode of disorientation that Paul arrived at a place
called Troas. This was over the water from modern-day Greece,
and it was here that God intervened. There are a number of factors
to note relating to this intervention which not only applied to Paul
but also apply to us. Because we, too, can find ourselves at 'Troas',
having no clear sense of direction regarding 'beyond the now'.

The first of these factors was that God knew the direction that
Paul needed to take and was therefore stopping him from taking
the wrong one. Luke's account in Acts 16 describes how this
worked out:

Paul and his companions travelled throughout the region of
Phrygia and Galatia, having been kept by the Holy Spirit
from preaching the word in the province of Asia. When they
came to the border of Mysia, they tried to enter Bithynia,
but the Spirit of Jesus would not allow them to. So they
passed by Mysia and went down to Troas.

(Acts 16:6–8)

Attempts to preach and continue ministry in those specific areas
of Asia and then Bithynia somehow didn't happen, and no

guidance was given when Paul and his friends were travelling around Phrygia and Galatia.

It is interesting to see that Paul clearly discerned God being behind these 'no entry' signs that he experienced. In subsequently writing to the Christians in Thessalonica, he stated that he was prevented from carrying out his intention of visiting them: 'For we wanted to come to you – certainly I, Paul, did, again and again – but Satan blocked our way' (1 Thessalonians 2:18). No details are provided of the actual form by which God, or Satan, prevented Paul from moving in a particular direction or destination. However, God's action was both identified and effective. It may have seemed a rather 'negative spin' to put on that intervention but it was still a valid means by which to get Paul and his companions heading in the right direction. It was also an intervention that was experienced over a period of time.

STOPPED BY GOD

God still has the ability to stop us pursuing a particular course of action, even if it leaves us (at least for a time) wondering what we should be doing. This is something I once experienced with a somewhat down-to-earth issue: work being done on my house. I had a small garden at the back of my terraced property and was thinking about the possibility of having a conservatory built on it. This would have involved considerable cost and disruption. I spent much time weighing up the advantages and disadvantages but was unable to feel ready to go ahead with the project. It dawned on me that the source of this unease was God. The evidence for this arose when my next-door neighbour leaned over the back garden fence some weeks later and casually informed me that he was embarking on a major rebuild of the back of his house! This included an attic conversion and kitchen extension, either of which would have wreaked havoc on my proposed (mainly glass) conservatory! I was very relieved – and grateful to God – that I had not gone ahead at that time. God once spoke through one of His prophets to assure His people (and us) of His intervention when taking the wrong direction: 'Whether you turn to the right or to the left, your ears will hear a voice behind you, saying, "This is the way; walk in it"' (Isaiah 30:21).

TAKING TIME

A second factor that was important in the situation that Paul faced was that he was prepared to take time and not be rushed into making a decision about the direction to be travelling. Although not clear about their ultimate destination, Paul was ready to go through a process (which involved time) in which 'doors' were 'closed', however many confronted him. Such an attitude is somewhat counter-intuitive for people in our own age. We are often placed under considerable pressure to make decisions and choices within a short time frame... if not sooner! The internet, a feature of everyday life, is not an environment that allows us to take time. We are frequently confronted with a series of screens requiring, if not seeming to demand, that we click a 'yes' or 'no' box (or similar) to move us on to the next part of the decision matrix. Online shopping is symptomatic of the scenario of pressing a key and instantly confirming a choice in nano-seconds.

It is clear that Paul was 'comfortable' in not pressing ahead until he sensed confirmation from God about situations. In that connection the narrative of Acts 16 subsequently showed that he involved others in this process: 'we got ready at once to leave for

Macedonia, concluding that God had called us to preach the gospel to them' (Acts 16:10, emphasis mine). By this time the group who accompanied Paul consisted of Silas, Timothy and Luke. Unlike the previous occasion (see Acts 15:36–41) when Paul had split up from Barnabas (on account of the latter wanting John Mark to accompany them) and had instead chosen Silas, there was clearly full agreement by everyone about the direction they were to take.

THE VISION

Next, Paul was in a 'place' to receive clear direction from God by means of a vision received at night regarding their destination. 'During the night Paul had a vision of a man of Macedonia standing and begging him, "Come over to Macedonia and help us"' (Acts 16:9). He was obviously looking to God to provide specific (and positive) guidance, and having this vision was sufficient for him, and his companions, to act upon.

At the same time, Paul was not holding to that vision as providing the finer details. As the situation subsequently unfolded, the first significant person that he met (in Philippi, their initial major stopping-off point) was not a man (as in the vision) but a woman. This was Lydia, a 'dealer in purple cloth', who was a worshipper of God and whose heart 'the Lord opened' in response to Paul's message (Acts 16:14). The next significant person whom Paul came across was also a woman, 'a female slave who had a spirit by which she predicted the future' (Acts 16:16). The 'help' that the 'man of Macedonia' had spoken about in the vision had perhaps indicated a smooth path ahead. But this also proved not to be the case. Paul ended up in prison after he delivered the female slave of her evil spirit, and her 'minders', now without an income from her clairvoyant abilities, organised a disturbance leading to Paul's arrest. But Paul had been satisfied that the vision was God's way of leading him in a clear direction.

ASSESSING

Finally, although Paul now knew the area where God was leading him, the actual location was not so obvious. So, again, Paul and his companions were prepared to take time to pursue their journey once they had arrived in the district of Macedonia. The account briefly describes that situation:

> From Troas we put out to sea and sailed straight for Samothrace, and the next day we went on to Neapolis. From there we travelled to Philippi, a Roman colony and the leading city of that district of Macedonia.
>
> (Acts 16:11–12)

As if to emphasise this aspect of taking time to assess their situation, the account concludes: 'And we stayed there [Philippi] several days.'

So, having travelled over to mainland Europe, Paul and his party progressed to Philippi, which was the first city reached when coming from the border. Being described as a 'colony' meant that it was a place commonly assigned to veteran soldiers of the Roman empire and was considered politically as an integral part of Rome with all the decrees of the emperor and senate being as binding there as in the capital.

ANOTHER OPTION

Paul usually engaged immediately in preaching and discussing with fellow Jews in the synagogue when he arrived at various destinations (as described, for example, in Acts 9:20; 9:28; 13:5; 13:13–15; 14:1), but he now hit a problem: there was no synagogue in Philippi. This meant that there was no obvious place in which to share the gospel about Jesus. However, there was also no obvious prohibition from God about doing so, such as Paul and his companions had previously experienced. So perhaps those 'several days' were spent assessing the practical as well as the spiritual situation. Perhaps, also, they were simply waiting for the Sabbath to arrive. Whereas a synagogue would be open daily, the alternative was likely to be more restricted. Paul, the narrative records, seemingly anticipated this other option: 'On the Sabbath we went outside the city gate to the river, where we expected to find a place of prayer' (Acts 16:13).

STEPPING OUT

Although it is not clear why there was no synagogue in that city – perhaps on account of the lack of Jewish men, or a legal prohibition – a 'place of prayer' (the term in the original language is 'oratory') was the alternative. Its location outside the city may have been a simple enclosure of stones, in a grove or under a tree, where there would be a convenient place for worship. Instead of finding men, Paul found a group of women with whom he and his companions sat down and began to talk. Not all of these women were Jewish. The one named Lydia (mentioned above) was a 'worshipper of God' (Acts 16:14), meaning that she was a proselyte – a Gentile who believed in the true God and followed the teaching of Scripture. She wasn't actually from Philippi, being from the city of Thyatira. But she listened and, in responding to God, was subsequently baptised together with 'the members of her household' (16:15). In comparison with previous experiences this situation initially may not have looked particularly promising. But from small beginnings – action taken on that day to 'step out' as the culmination of previously following God's direction – a church was born and the good news about Jesus was planted in Europe for the first time. 'One day' can make a huge difference in your life... it's made a huge difference in the past:

- One day a monk stepped out and nailed his objections to church practices to the church door in Wittenberg. The action of Martin Luther in 1517 was integral to the Reformation which impacted the world.

- One day a man stepped into a meeting room in Aldersgate, London, and had a life-changing encounter with God. The conversion of John Wesley in 1738 resulted in him being used by God to bring revival to the UK and beyond, the impact of which is still felt today.

- One day a young Welsh girl stepped out of her house to walk barefoot for 20 miles so that she could get hold of a Welsh Bible she had sought after. The action of Mary Jones in 1820 galvanised others to see the need to make the Bible more widely available. The subsequent foundation of the British and Foreign Bible Society – responding to Mary Jones' action – has resulted in countless millions of people receiving a copy of the Scriptures in their mother tongue.

- One day a British army general deliberately dismounted from his horse outside the walls of Jerusalem and walked through the Jaffa Gate. It was December 1917 and the action of General Sir Edmund Allenby, leading the allied armies, marked the end of centuries of oppression of foreign powers over that city. It eventually led to the founding of the nation state of Israel, regarded by many Christians as integral to the Second Coming of Jesus as King of kings.

* * *

REFLECTION

Grounds for hope (as seen in this chapter):

- God is well able to stop us from taking the wrong direction.
- God brings confirmation, in time, regarding the direction we need to take.
- There will come a day when direction will come from God.
- God's direction doesn't necessarily mean that we have all the details (so we don't need to be concerned if these are not what we anticipated).

POINTS TO PONDER

1. Why do we sometimes feel frustrated when we can't reach an immediate decision in a significant area of our lives? Tick as many boxes as apply.

   We don't want to 'hang around' but would rather get going ☐

   There is a sense that God is remote and not guiding us ☐

   We feel that it reflects on our relationship with God ☐

   It makes us wonder if we misunderstood previous guidance ☐

   There is a feeling that others have, in some way, confused us ☐

2. Why do we need to realise that God's direction of our lives consists of 'shutting doors' as well as 'opening' them?

3. How can we distinguish between God's work of stopping us making a particular choice, and Satan trying to obstruct us from moving ahead in the way that God wants?

4. What is the value of taking time to make decisions and not being forced to rush into choices?

5. Why is it important to understand that God can guide us through many different means, including those which may be more 'supernatural' as well as those less dramatic?

6. In what aspect of your life are you needing to get ready for the day when you must step out in a specific way as directed by God?

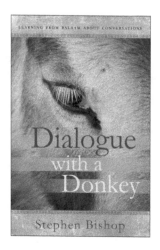

DIALOGUE WITH A DONKEY

Learning from Balaam about conversations

Stephen Bishop

A talking donkey and sword-wielding angel are the images most commonly associated with the Old Testament character of Balaam. Yet the significance and relevance of this account seem to be rarely considered.

"Dialogue with a Donkey" aims to open up this extraordinary story by looking at other conversations that were taking place… and which continue to do so. The compelling force of words to specifically direct, challenge, influence, affirm and develop people's lives are considered through Balaam's successive utterances. These pronouncements brought a divine perspective to the Israelites at that time. As this book advocates, we also need to hear what God is saying, breaking through all surrounding voices. It also underlines how Balaam's words reached a climax in pointing to Jesus who continues powerfully speaking into our darkness.

The stubborn donkey ends up being the means by which other people had God's life-giving word brought to them. We also need to hear such words. Are we listening?

ISBN 9781909824256
5.5 x 8.5" Paperback
Published by Zaccmedia

FLEECES, FEARS AND FLAMES

Gideon – Learning to connect with God

Stephen Bishop

Gideon is a well-known Bible character. His exploits in leading just three hundred men to defeat a huge invading army has inspired many people when faced with situations which are 'against-all-odds'. But how did it occur? Where was God in this scenario? How does this account relate to us?

'Fleeces, fears and flames' explores the Book of Judges in order to examine these ques-tions. Written in a down-to-earth manner, it looks at God connecting with Gideon despite his fears and fleece-laying doubts, then breaking through such frailty to release his power as seen in those flames. But it also shows that God is able to connect and work in our lives however daunting the challenges confronting us!

Suitable for individual reflection or group discussion, this material includes questions and a focus at the end of each main chapter to help connect the Biblical narrative in a personal way.

ISBN 9781909824492
5.5 x 8.5" Paperback
Published by Zaccmedia

FOCUSING BEYOND THE HORIZON
Samuel – Learning to see God's Perspective
Stephen Bishop

We relate to our surroundings by sight and sound. Together with our other senses we are able to interact with people and situations. But are these enough? Is more happening around us than we understand? Are we missing out on a further perspective?

This book, 'Focusing beyond the horizon,' looks at the Biblical character of Samuel in the Old Testament. Described as a prophet, or "seer", he saw more than the material world around him, being enabled to understand something of God's bigger picture.

Looking at the way in which God worked in Samuel's life, each bite-sized chapter in this material explores some of these factors and how we can also understand our world from God's viewpoint.

ISBN 9781909824737
5.5 x 8.5" Paperback
Published by Zaccmedia

TIME: FULL STOP OR QUESTION MARK?

Looking at God, Timing and Us
Stephen Bishop

'Time,' often termed as the 'fourth dimension,' affects us all. Whatever our status, background or ability, it totally influences our actions and attitudes. But is it 'non-negotiable'? Does it exert complete control? Is 'time' the ultimate 'full-stop'?

The Bible records the eternal God intervening in the affairs of this world and individual lives. Looking at the different ways in which such intervention took place, this book considers events when God broke through our conception of time, and how Jesus exampled a life outside of its limitations.

Suitable for personal reflection or group discussion, this Biblical perspective also considers how we can experience God working beyond those constraints of time. It doesn't necessarily provide answers, but perhaps changes 'time' to a 'question mark'!

ISBN 9781911211617
5.5 x 8.5" Paperback
Published by Zaccmedia

Lightning Source UK Ltd.
Milton Keynes UK
UKHW01f1028110718
325520UK00006B/266/P